KW-550-322

Contemporary
sociology of
the school

General editor
JOHN EGGLESTON

The sociology of educational inequality

CONTEMPORARY SOCIOLOGY
OF THE SCHOOL

PAUL BELLABY
The sociology of comprehensive schooling

BRIAN DAVIES
Social control and education

SARA DELAMONT
Interaction in the classroom

JOHN EGGLESTON
The ecology of the school

ERIC HOYLE
School organization and administration

COLIN LACEY
The socialization of teachers

PETER MUSGRAVE
The moral curriculum: a sociological analysis

PHILIP ROBINSON
Education and poverty

MICHAEL STUBBS
Language, schools and classrooms

WILLIAM TYLER
The sociology of educational inequality

TOM WHITESIDE
The sociology of educational innovation

Editor's introduction

Sociology has changed dramatically in the past decade. Sociologists have provided an ever increasing diversity of empirical and theoretical approaches that are advancing our understanding of the complexities of societies and their educational arrangements. It is now possible to see the over-simplification of the earlier sociological view of the world running smoothly with agreed norms of behaviour, with institutions and individuals performing functions that maintained society and where even conflict was restricted to 'agreed' areas. This normative view of society with its functionalist and conflict theories has now been augmented by a range of interpretative approaches in which the realities of human interaction have been explored by phenomenologists, ethnomethodologists and other reflexive theorists. Together they have emphasized the part that individual perceptions play in determining social reality and have challenged many of the characteristics of society that the earlier sociologists had assumed to be 'given'.

The new approaches have had striking effects upon the sociology of the school. Earlier work was characterized by a range of incompletely examined assumptions about such matters as ability, opportunity and social class. Sociologists asked how working class children could achieve in the schools like middle class children. Now they also ask how a social system defines class, opportunities and achievement. Such concepts and many others such as subjects, the curriculum and even schools themselves are seen to be products of the social system in which they exist. In this study of the school we can see with special clarity the ways in which individual teachers' and students' definitions of the situation help to determine its social arrangements; how perceptions of achievement can not only define achievement but also identify those who achieve; how expectations about schooling can determine the nature and evaluation of schools.

This series of volumes explores the main areas of the sociology of the school in which new understanding of events is now available. Each introduces the reader to the new interpretations, juxtaposes them against the longer standing perspectives and reappraises the contemporary practice of education and its consequences.

In each specialist authors develop their own analyses of central issues such as poverty, opportunity, comprehensive schooling, the language and interaction of the classroom, the teacher's role, the ecology of education, and ways in which education acts as an instrument of social control. The broad spectrum of themes and treatments is closely interrelated; it is offered to all who seek new illumination on the practice of education and to those who wish to know how contemporary sociological theory can be applied to educational issues.

In this volume William Tyler treats one of the most enduring themes in the sociology of education, the relationship of education to the structures of opportunity, privilege and social mobility in industrial society. He reviews the development of the debate since the turn of the century when both liberals and socialists thought that sweeping social change attended educational reform. With the aid of a wide range of contemporary research he sets out to show why such promises have not been fulfilled, against a background of changing definitions of equality, disadvantage and achievement. What has been the relationship between credentials and occupation? Is there a genetic basis to the cycle of disadvantage? Can schools ever play an effective role in restructuring opportunity and rewards? Can a compensatory policy be linked to a voucher scheme? Can we ever equalize outcomes?

William Tyler, who has undertaken extensive research in the sociology of educational opportunity in Britain and the US, has written a book which imposes a new pattern on existing knowledge and sets the stage for future advances in the sociology of educational opportunity.

John Eggleston

1

The causal structure of educational inequality

It is difficult in a time of heated educational debate to view the general question of educational inequality dispassionately. It is perhaps more difficult to put forward solutions that contradict the very premises on which such debates are held and at the same time provide a promise for abolishing the inequities of the present system. The following argument is therefore designed both to guide the reader through the current literature on educational inequality, and to direct him past the pitfalls and fallacies of contemporary dogma. If this sounds a little condescending, and rather too much like an assertion of the superiority of a 'value free' sociology over 'ideology', then it is so only because we are at present in great danger of repeating the mistakes of the past and, like the Bourbons, incapable of either learning anything or forgetting anything.

The following discussion therefore represents an attempt to get beyond the pessimism and resignation that swept educational circles at the beginning of this decade, and to expose the fallacies behind the extremes of ideological thinking which such defeatism appears to have engendered. In this attempt to reassert the relevance of an empirical social science to educational practice it will appear that the future holds many possibilities for a radical policy that is consistent with the social-democratic experiments of the post-war years, but which gives some evidence of having learnt by past mistakes.

In order to arrive at the point of formulating new directions for policy we will first have to examine carefully the main issues in this field. This first chapter will trace the road to the present impasse in educational thinking and identify the main models of educational inequality in terms of their causal networks. The remainder of the book will attempt to examine the validity of these models in the light of the most recent evidence. A chapter apiece is therefore devoted to looking at the main areas of debate – the relations between credentials and jobs, the quality of the school environment, the acquisition of IQ and the effects of social background on attainment.

The reader may discern, amidst the discussion of the evidence, threads of an argument which are pulled together in the final chapter. Briefly stated, this argument asserts the overriding importance of structural and material constraints on educational attainment. It depreciates in turn the significance of school organization and teaching styles, of inherited ability and of the cultural influence of the home as the basis for a systematic attack on educational inequalities. If this emphasis on structural and material factors sounds at all Marxist, then it should be pointed out now that the evidence also fails to support the simplistic formulae of the 'new left'. Instead of claiming that such constraints are inevitable features of the social relations of advanced capitalism, I suggest that they may be deeply embedded in any society that has a complex division of labour. It is hoped therefore that the reader will be eventually persuaded to view the problems of education in a different light, and come perhaps to appreciate just how much more needs to be known before true educational equality is extended to all children.

What is educational inequality? When people speak of inequality in education they may mean several things. They may mean, for example, that some children can read better than others for their age, and are more likely to stay on at school and go on to university. They may mean, on the other hand, that some children come from families that give them certain advantages such as encyclopedias, visits to art galleries and museums and help with their homework. A possible, though perhaps more unusual, meaning could be that some children are able to read at higher levels than others of the same age because they were born that way. In this case any advantage would be a natural or innate one.

More often than not, however, educational inequality is about the advantages that come from different experiences and stimulation that the school provides. Some people believe that sending a child to a fee-paying school will give him a headstart in life. Because of the 'better' or more academic educational climate of the school it is claimed that the child will learn faster, stay on longer and pick up credentials that will increase his lifetime earnings. On the non-academic side it is believed that such a child may be more likely to make friends who in later life could help him to obtain a high status and well-paying occupation.

Let us go through these different meanings of educational inequality again and give each of them the term that is used by writers in this field. The first kind of inequality is that of *achievement*, as shown in different levels of competence or skill in school subjects such as reading, arithmetic or knowledge of history or geography. The second refers to inequality in educational *background*, usually in the family which in turn may be related to the neighbourhood, the occupational group of the father, the region or an ethnic group. The third inequality is that of *aptitude* or *ability*, that is of potential for learning. Although many would disagree with the claim that this is inborn, there is no doubt that it remains fairly constant after a certain age. The fourth type of inequality is that of *school environment*. This is the area that is most hotly discussed and debated because it is the one that people feel is both the most important and most easily removed. It may refer to the type of teaching, facilities or curriculum that the school offers, or it may refer to its non-academic advantages – its 'snob' appeal – reflected in the manners, the accent and the social standing of the child's friendship group.

The two remaining types of inequality are concerned with tangible outcomes of education. First of all there are *credentials* which are indicated by the level and quality of examination results, or simply by a piece of paper to prove that an individual has attended an institution for a certain period of time. Finally there are *life chances* which refer here specifically to status and income. These are to a large extent influenced by the type, quality and duration of schooling one has received. Some sociologists claim that this influence is increasing and that most of the differences between people will soon be almost entirely determined by their educational success. This is sometimes called 'educational stratification' and is believed by many writers to be a necessary characteristic of modern society.

It may appear then that it is very difficult to use the term 'educational inequality' because it can refer to so many things – potential, opportunity, outcomes and rewards. This should not disturb us, however, since writers in education or in sociology usually make it clear which type of inequality they are referring to. What is more important than the particular uses of the term are the relationships that are implied and direction of a writer's bias in *explaining* one particular kind of inequality. In fact, it is almost impossible to use the term 'educational inequality' in one sense without at the same time implying how it may be related to or connected with all the others. It is for this reason that we have to unravel the causal structure of different models of educational success in order to see the full implications of a particular usage. Let us look at two such models.

Let us suppose that all children are born unequal in their capacity to learn in a normal school environment. If this is so, then we should not be at all surprised that they drop out of the formal educational system at different rates. The first type of inequality explains or accounts for the latter. In addition, if we were to imagine that there is very little difference in the kinds of environments to which very bright and very dull children are exposed, then the initial differences in ability would shine through all the more clearly in outcomes. To go even one stage further, we could link innate ability to family background. This would give us a very strong explanation of all types of educational inequality indeed.

From this explanation or set of explanations we could propose a model of occupational structure which over a period of time becomes almost completely determined by family background. Rich and intellectually competent parents would pass on all their advantages to their children, who would succeed in the school system and in later life and ultimately give their own children a similar headstart. In such a model biological inheritance of ability is the 'engine' of inequality, since family, school and work simply reinforce genetic endowments. Here it should be noted that the equalization of environments would only make inherited inequality more prominent. This is, in fact, the model of 'the meritocracy' that has been proposed by Richard Herrnstein (1971; 1973).

Let us, however, propose a different set of relationships, in which social and family background rather than inherited ability is the driving force. We might start off with the premise that family background is a more important determinant of educational success than is ability. We could say, too, that ability is in any case more the result of a child's home background and early educational experiences than of his biological inheritance. In fact, we could claim that inequalities of all kinds are simply reflections of existing patterns of privilege and power. Children from advantaged homes will, therefore, be more likely to have a happier and more rewarding school life. When it comes to finding a job, what these children may have learned at school will not be considered as important by employers as the attitudes, deportment and general manner that they will have acquired. Credentials then may be seen as devices for 'screening' out applicants who do not have the 'right' background.

This is the 'radical' or 'class conflict' model of educational inequality and is to be contrasted with the first. Just as the supposed equalization of opportunity to talent characterized the 'meritocratic' model it is the inevitable tendency of the class structure to restrict opportunity and to define talent in its own terms that marks this model off. Children from poorer backgrounds never have, in the words of the Newsom Report (1963), 'an equal opportunity for acquiring intelligence'. They are, more often than not, labelled as 'ineducable', passed into schools or 'streams' that do not provide them with positive learning environments and where the expectation is that they will leave early. This model is represented, according to its adherents, in the English 'tripartite' system of secondary schooling. The 1944 Act which instituted the early division of children into three ability categories has done little, according to them, to alter the truth of Tawney's (1931) dictum that 'the hereditary curse of English education is its organization along the lines of class'.

These are not, however, the only two possible models of educational inequality. There are, for example, some writers who believe that a system that restricts opportunity is not only inevitable but indeed desirable. It is in the nature of things, according to them, that the children of the privileged classes are better endowed intellectually, go to 'better' schools and dominate the élite institutions of learning. However, the thought of a 'meritocracy', where the class structure was subservient to the educational system, frightens such writers. Those who hold this model would rather small changes were made, where the culture of the élite is not threatened by too hasty meritocratic reforms and where the institutional bulwarks of privilege, the fee-paying and selective schools, are largely left alone.

It may seem rather strange, then, that this very conservative approach should often call upon geneticist and biological arguments in order to justify selective forms of secondary education. This is however the case, as a perusal of the *Black Papers* (1969–75), four collections of conservative educational writings, will show. The alliance between the conservative and the geneticist case is probably only a very superficial one since the contributors to these publications were united by the common fear of comprehensive education. In fact, the 'conservative' position is much closer to the 'radical' model mentioned above than it is to the purely 'meritocratic' in its description of how the school and class system operates to provide a stable cycle of inequality. Adherents of both the 'conservative' and the 'radical' models would agree that intelligence is not a 'natural' talent but rather something conferred by society. In the case of the conservatives, talent is seen to be produced by centuries of selective breeding and is a reflection of culture rather than, as 'meritocrats' would see it, of natural selection. Radicals, of course, would deny any claim that biological intelligence may be 'cultivated' by the élites, but they are close to the conservatives in their claim that all 'natural' qualities have a social origin.

We have so far analysed the causal structure of three approaches to educational inequality – the 'meritocratic', the 'radical' and the 'conservative' (or 'traditional élitist'). As we have seen, the unravelling of the bundles of relationships between the different types of inequality has produced some rather unexpected results. This has been because, instead of identifying approaches by their stance on a particular issue, such as comprehensive schooling or the inheritance of ability, we have tried to base them on the particular model of social inequality that each puts forward. Simply labelling sociological models by their ideological or political complexion can lead, as we shall see, to unsatisfactory results – particularly when we come to testing them against some empirical study.

The *Black Papers* are again a case in point, not merely because they tend to represent the views of people who are opposed to 'progressive' educational tendencies but because they present probably as many different views as there are contributors. We will find gradations of opinion, therefore, rather than sharp contrast, even on the political 'right' of the debate about educational inequality. A collection of statements united under the common cause of resisting a particular kind of school reform may disguise rather than reveal fundamental differences in the explanatory model being used.

Of particular interest here is the gradation of viewpoints within the 'school' that holds to a hereditary model of intelligence. Rather than agreeing with Herrnstein that the tendency of the 'meritocracy' is towards a kind of caste system, many would claim that the inheritance of ability produces a large degree of interchange between the classes (or social mobility) from one generation to the next. From this perspective it would seem that selection by measured ability promotes rather than denies educational and social opportunity. These people would strenuously refute, with a host of empirical studies, the claim that there is a restricted 'pool of ability' which explains the different class rates of achievement and success. They would make a plea for more rigorous testing combined with specific kinds of treatment for different kinds of aptitude. It is possible then to hold to a *weak* relationship between family background and inherited ability and at the same time put forward a *strong* relationship between individual inheritance and educational chances. The tensions in this model become apparent in the claims for and against mixed ability teaching, particularly in the comprehensive school. This explanatory model may be called 'evolutionary liberal' and has been the most widely supported in the immediate post-war years in Britain and in other western countries.

Just as there may be tensions within the ideological 'right' of the inequality debate, it would be foolish to suppose that all those of the left support a simple version of the 'radical' or 'class conflict' model outlined above. Here again there are wide differences, in the actual degree to which education is seen to offer a ladder of opportunity, however restricted, to the children of the working and lower classes. As for the biological élitists, we have liberal or 'softer' versions of the ways in which cycles of inequality are maintained. These are more compatible with the policies of intervention of the modern welfare state, and again rely on a gradualist model of social change. If intelligence is not primarily inherited, then it may be possible to use the educational system as a means of compensating for the 'deprived' environment of the home. This model may be called the 'compensatory liberal'. It tended, as we shall see below, to replace the 'evolutionary liberal' and was the major support for thinking and policy in the early 1960s.

There are, however, much more fundamental differences among those who believe that intelligence and success tend to follow existing patterns of inequality in family background. On the one hand, we have those who claim that there are important educational advantages that go with the 'culture' of the home, its life style, its types of speech, and the value that it places on educational success. On the other, there are those who say that these cultural advantages merely disguise – or reflect – more fundamental differences between families: their relationship to the means of production, their material resources and the power of the father in the work hierarchy. Once these inequalities are removed, these writers claim, there will no longer be any of the other dimensions of educational inequality. They often deny that there is any separate 'culture of poverty' or that the middle-class life style confers an intrinsic disposition to learning. Of course, teachers may *treat* middle-class children differently and this may end up in their doing better at school, but this is only a product of the original inequality in power relationships, and in material conditions in their respective backgrounds.

It is here that we may introduce the two different approaches to the classification of family background. These may be arranged along the lines of class on the one hand, and of 'socio-economic status' (SES) on the other. They parallel very closely the two approaches to a conflict model of educational inequality outlined in the previous paragraph. Those who place a strong emphasis on the cultural advantages of the home and on parental encouragement tend to see social inequality in terms of life style, housing, consumption patterns and the education of both parents. All of these characteristics, strongly related to income and social standing, are what sociologists call 'socio-economic status' (SES). These must be contrasted with the characteristics that accompany the family's place in the hierarchy of wealth and power. While the first approach leads to a gradual *continuum* of inequality, the second leads to sharp contrasts in social groups between the rich and the poor, the powerful and the dominated. It is no wonder then that even though it is possible to see education as a carrier of inequality in both models, there may be enormous differences in prescribing a suitable cure.

Some of the most bitter debates in the area of educational inequality have been concerned with the formulation of policies that may break into the cycles of educational inequality. All theorists admit that the home environment does have a great deal to do with educational achievement and examination success, but there is now very little agreement about the assumptions that should guide policy. Do we assume, for example, that a type of 'cultural deprivation' exists, that it has a real and independent influence on educational outcomes and that it is amenable to change? Or do we see such 'deprivation' as a part of a larger problem of inequality and exploitation in capitalist society and try to change the material and political condition of the poor? Would it help, in other words, to take the children of an unemployed labourer to the Opera once a month and to teach them more standard forms of English? Finally, should we see 'deprivation', like success, as a relative thing and say that the only way out of the problem is to see it through the eyes of the people whose lives are to be researched and reorganized? In this case a lot of the preconceptions that we hold about reforming education may be seen to reflect a middle-class set of values. If we did wish to avoid the problem of cultural insensitivity, how far should we go towards maintaining the integrity of those cultures and life styles that are different from those of the 'mainstream' or dominant types?

These are all hotly debated issues among those who do not subscribe to élitist, let alone genetic, models of inequality. It is not surprising, then, that the student in the area may feel a little confused by all of the competing approaches, models and theories.

Let us stop for a moment and try to reconsider the main explanations of educational inequality put forward so far. First of all, we saw that each explanation has a type of 'wholeness', that is, each kind of inequality is usually seen to have some effect or influence on every other type. We then saw it was possible to build up very 'strong', not to say extreme, explanations by adding one link of the chain systematically to another. Indeed, it is possible in these 'strong' models to see education as a kind of a 'photocopying' machine of the existing system of stratification. This was done by making measured intelligence *or* family background (or both) the driving force of the machine. We then saw that less extreme (or weaker) models of explanation could be built up by detaching intelligence from family background on the one hand, and from its biological inheritance on the other.

This gave us our five main models: (1) the 'meritocratic' model (in Herrnstein's sense) where inherited ability is the motive force; (2) the 'class conflict' model where the existing patterns of material and cultural inequality dominate all of the others; (3) the 'traditional élitist' or 'conservative' model which combines both genetic and environmental explanations of inequality; (4) the 'evolutionary liberal' model which is similar to the 'meritocratic' model but proposes a weak connection between intelligence and family background; (5) the 'compensatory liberal' model which resembles the 'class conflict' model but proposes that school environment and credentials can significantly improve the life chances of working-class children.

These five models give us a good general map of approaches to policy and thinking in all western countries, if not all industrialized countries, throughout this century. Each, as we shall see in the following short historical account, has enjoyed a period of initial popularity, and often of revival.

The evolution of the inequality debate

The most striking aspect of the evolution of the debate on educational inequality in western countries over this century has been the rapidity with which ideas have been diffused, rejected and modified. This has happened at all levels of debate, from the highly academic to that of the popular press. What is also striking in this is the way in which popular debate has fed off recent and often esoteric arguments among social scientists. This is seen, for example, in the almost instantaneous publication of some of Arthur Jensen's views by the southern press of the United States, or in the United Kingdom by the publicity given to the 'failure' of a comprehensive system or of 'progressive' teaching methods. Thanks largely to a huge amount of advertising, Christopher Jencks' *Inequality* (discussed below) reached the bestseller lists in English-speaking countries, despite the fact that its arguments are based on the interpretation of a fairly sophisticated statistical diagram.

The flow of ideas has not been in the one direction, however. Very often it is the ferment at the popular level that provides the inspiration for social research. At the end of the second war the political and moral context of social reform laid the basis for a thriving sociology of education in the western democracies. Social science was to provide the unique expertise to monitor the effects of legislation, to indicate the impediments to progress and to initiate new proposals and fresh definitions of injustice. The political awareness that all is not well with a particular reform can spark off enormous controversy in the learned literature, as seen for example in the debate over bussing during the 1972 Presidential campaign in the US. Very often the flow of ideas is circular, however, with the implementation of a social theory into policy, its consequent modification in practice and a further academic debate as the proponents of the original idea are challenged by new evidence. Such a process is to be observed in the history of educational selection by measured ability in the pre- and post-war years in Britain.

In recent years, as we will see, some very exciting yet disturbing developments have taken place within the inequality debate. So confused and heated have the arguments and counter-arguments become that many people have turned sceptical at the hope that there can ever be a dividing line between politics, ideology and social science. The liberal pact of the post-war years has been superseded in the 1970s by a number of debates, all around contentious issues such as 'bussing', 'comprehensives', 'voucher' schemes and the racial 'gap' in IQ scores. It is small wonder that outsiders to these debates may feel that claims to objectivity, rationality and even truth are often suspect. At the same time many may not consider the claim that we should abandon these criteria is altogether acceptable, no matter how much we may 'hedge our bets' by recognizing the limitations of our case. The fact that 'moral conviction usually prevails over inconclusive statistics' (Jenkins in *The Guardian*) should not blind us to the validity of all evidence.

If there is a 'war of the models' in the contemporary debate about educational inequality, then it has certainly not been cooled by the rate at which social scientific findings are produced, disseminated and consumed. If anything, this has accelerated the tendency for people to read and see only those findings which fit in with their own framework of explanation. It has also led to the clash of viewpoint within particular 'models', the modification or refinement of perspective, the revival of long-forgotten debates and the development of new varieties of explanation. This has particularly affected the 'class conflict' model as seen above in the problems that arise out of dealing with poverty and 'cultural deprivation'. How, in fact, did the present confusion arise? How can inequality be explained? What can we do about it? These are the questions which we shall now consider.

Although the main impetus to educational reform in western countries has not been at all clear, it has generally grown out of the concern for opportunity and efficiency. The desire to reduce inequality in opportunity that one reads about in public documents such as the White Paper on Educational Reconstruction (1943), though apparently a straightforward motive, is less so when we subject it to scrutiny. In the first place, it often appears that opportunity simply means the access to resources. In this case one would have been satisfied if equal amounts of money were allocated to children of different classes. This would not have been sufficient of course because education, as distinct from other social services, is not given by *need* but by *merit*. Those who succeed will always tend to stay on longer at school. If merit has to be rewarded, however, what weight should it be given, particularly in deciding the point at which the rate of scholastic success between the classes has been equalized? This leads us immediately into a debate about the kinds of rewards that are appropriate for a certain level of success on the one hand, and about the origins of ability and motivation on the other. True equality of opportunity, then, may reside in either breaking down the links between scholastic and material success, or in abolishing the environmental influences that cause cognitive inequality. These questions are obvious enough and yet they have often been ignored when people speak of equal opportunity as though it were always a simple matter of equalizing expenditures across regions or socio-economic groups.

The simple desire for more social equality in provision, though a large influence on the policies of this century, has not been the only mainspring of reform. Possibly of greater importance has been the belief that educational expansion represents a necessary condition for economic growth and that the greater the educational budget, the higher will be the efficiency and adaptability of the workforce. Since this is presumably connected with the higher rewards that individuals will receive in terms of status and income, it can be easily seen how attractive this argument could be to those who wished to increase social as well as educational opportunity in a society. By combining the two types of reform it might appear that social progress and economic growth could be made compatible.

These two strains of reasoning have been implied in most educational reform. Manpower arguments have mingled with the egalitarian cause to produce a liberal credo that educational expansion could eventually cure poverty, promote a more able, skilled and mobile workforce, and perhaps even in the long run break down class distinctions as they have traditionally been defined. Since this line of argument has not been the property of the 'left' or of the 'right' in western countries, it is probably why the assumptions on which it was based were for so long unexamined. The failure of education to 'deliver the goods' has led in most part to the present confusion of policy and the tendency towards a rejection of both of the 'liberal' models and the proliferation of the more extreme kinds of explanation. The fact that none of the three 'extreme' models outlined above present any better explanation of educational inequality than do the two 'liberal' ones does not apparently affect their popularity.

The origins of the 'liberal' beliefs in the economic and social benefits of educational equality can be traced back to the nineteenth century. Halsey (1975a) specifically mentions in his analysis of this theory of 'educational embourgoisement', the contribution of Alfred Marshall. Every man could lead the life of the middle-class gentleman if society were ordered about the life of learning. The fruits of industry would increase, and there would be a gradual attenuation of class differences and rivalries. There was, however, no middle-class premium on such theories. As Brian Simon's (1960) historical analysis of the education of the English working class shows, the faith in the social and egalitarian benefits of education were just as strong at the other end of the social spectrum. It was this faith that was carried over into the theories of the Fabian reformers of the first part of the century that did so much to shape the educational policies of the welfare state. Education could be seen as the main agent of gradual social change, where ability and industry would profitably replace hereditary privilege.

The inequality debate since the second world war

The hope was realized in the spread of secondary education to all classes by the middle of the century in most western countries. In Britain the 1944 Act enshrined the principle that the socialists and radicals had demanded for nearly half a century. In the United States the idea of universal, or near-universal, secondary schooling had been accepted much earlier and was greatly assisted by the effects of the 1930s' depression. The organization of education in both countries, though apparently greatly different – the former being 'handed down', the latter being much more of a 'folk' institution – was dominated by similar norms of selection and allocation to jobs. In both countries the curriculum was geared to three types of students – the academic, the vocational and the 'general'. Whether the organization was accomplished by the use of 'tracks', 'streams' or separate schools, the social implication of educational allocation appeared to be much the same.

After the second world war, despite the openness of access to secondary education by ability, it was soon obvious that the promise of change in educational and social opportunity was not to be so easily realized. Even though, as Floud, Halsey and Martin (1956) showed in two English districts, the differences in measured ability did account for most of the class rates of selection to grammar schools, it was still true that these rates were virtually unchanged by the 1944 Act. In order to account for them one would need a theory of how intelligence was acquired, that is, an explanation of the environmental and hereditary mechanisms that produce differential ability between the classes. This was an important, though largely academic, concern of the 1950s (Halsey, 1958; Burt, 1959).

The failure of the educational reforms to alter the rates of success between children of different family backgrounds was corroborated in many studies in Britain, the US and Canada. 'Dropping out' or 'early leaving' was highly related to socio-economic background, and its explanation seemed elusive. In Britain there were numerous studies, and government reports, which documented the statistical side of the problem. The best known of the studies are those of Little and Westergaard (1964) and J. W. B. Douglas (1964). Of the government reports, *Early Leaving* (1954) and *15 to 18* (Crowther, 1959) present some of the most telling evidence, while the Robbins Report (1963) showed how the inequalities in selection were magnified in the proportions reaching higher education. The evidence from these studies suggests that the son of a professional worker had roughly eleven times the chance of selection to a grammar school as did the son of a semi-skilled worker and about twenty-five times the chance of going to a university.

The most obvious target for reform in a system which maintains a large degree of class bias is likely to be the institutional apparatus itself. In Britain, as distinct from the other English-speaking countries, it was much easier to isolate the culprit in the selective school system and the iniquitous test of the 11+. The selective school system not only concentrated the university bias of curriculum, the physical and professional endowment of the institution, and the academic ethos of the peer-group, but it apparently linked these to a restrictive cycle of privilege. It appeared that the abolition of such a system would perforce open up the avenues of higher learning to those who were excluded by a class-biased and unreliable test, equalize the distribution of teaching skills and physical resources, and perhaps even increase the rates of social as well as of educational inequality. Anthony Crosland, who was to be instrumental in implementing the first national reform towards comprehensive schooling, wrote in 1956 that 'all schools will be more and more socially mixed; all will provide routes to the University and to every type of occupation, from the highest to the lowest. Then very slowly, Britain may cease to be the most class-ridden country in the world' (quoted by Ford, 1969).

The attack on selective schooling was, however, only one of the ways in which the geneticist and 'evolutionary' basis of the post-war reforms could be ignored or replaced by environmental explanations. There was, for example, the demonstration from the Crowther Report and the Robbins Report that the possibility that a restricted 'pool of ability' could lie behind the slope of class chances in higher education was patently absurd. This refutation relied on the fact that misallocation of even a small percentage of children from each class would inevitably produce a higher amount of 'wasted' talent among the children of the most numerous groups. Thus Jean Floud (1961) was able to demonstrate from the National Service Survey that there were untapped 'reserves of ability' among boys of the second highest ability group (i.e. 20 per cent of the age group). Of these, two-thirds had left school at the minimum age, and one half of these 'early leavers' were the sons of skilled manual workers. The Robbins Report (1963) corroborated this analysis with the finding that even among the top group (boys of IQ in excess of 130) those from non-manual backgrounds had about twice the chance of entering a degree level course over those from manual families.

The pursuit of environmental arguments for the educational failure was accelerated during the 1960s by alarm at the economic costs of such high rates of wastage. It was here that a shift in the terms of the debate took place and where the 'evolutionary' basis of liberal policy was replaced by an explicit 'compensatory' one. Here the arguments against educational selection merged with attacks on the concept of 'innate' intelligence. If only enough resources were reallocated, if only some intervention were made before the child came to school, if only expansion were made in colleges and universities, if only the right teaching techniques were used, then the class differential would be reduced. This type of debate was more likely when there was a case for spending on educational as against other kinds of services. This case was supplied by a very influential school of economic thought in the 1960s, known as 'human capital' or 'human investment'.

This economic theory put forward the close connection between a nation's productivity and its human resources in terms of the levels of skill, ability and education of the population (Bowman, 1966). The nation that failed to invest in these would inevitably suffer, since knowledge was the key to industrial, and indeed military, superiority. Mere investment in plant and machinery without a commensurate development of human resources would not be enough. This thinking was inspired to a large degree by the computer 'revolution' which appeared to provide unparalleled opportunities for the extension of human intelligence. Not only was the development of the information and knowledge industry central to national economy, the possibilities for learning and teaching that the new technology offered were themselves immense. The educational system, as well as becoming central to the allocation of children to their future positions, was also the nation's major growth industry. Because of the hopes that education was to fulfil the needs of personal mobility, of increased social opportunity and affluence, of national economic growth and self-sufficiency, it is no wonder that critics like Ivan

Illich (1970) were, by the end of the decade, able to call it the new 'secular religion'.

In such a climate of opinion it was difficult to argue a simple 'evolutionary' case, that ability is fixed at birth. The orthodoxy in the western democracies at this time was overwhelmingly environmentalist. The rapid growth in the post-war capitalist economies, coupled with higher rates of geographical mobility and of educational attainment, all appeared to demonstrate that equality was largely a matter of opportunity. If this was the case, and if the 'human capital' arguments were correct, then the existence of cultures which somehow restrict educational opportunity must be seen not only as damaging to the ideal of social equality, but as blights to national efficiency. The culture of the working class, and of minority groups therefore, become 'dysfunctional' and must be corrected. Programmes of intervention must be devised, investigations of linguistic 'deficit' must be carried out and more money must be spent on teaching, schools and teacher education, so that the cognitive disadvantage transmitted by these backgrounds can be stamped out for good. The programmes aimed at eliminating the effects of cultural deprivation can be seen as a link between the manpower needs of the advanced industrial state and the perceived failure of the 'evolutionary' model to provide an adequate explanation of educational attainment.

Of particular interest in the progress of this debate is the interpretation given to the theories of educability being propounded at the time by Basil Bernstein. In the rather oversimplified popular version, it seemed that Bernstein was proposing a linguistic theory of failure. The working-class child was limited to the 'here and now' by his linguistic experience (the 'restricted code'), while the middle-class child could rise above his immediate situation and reflect on underlying principles and remote patterns of causation (the 'elaborated code'). It is not to the present point whether this is in fact what Bernstein was saying, but this indeed was the construction that was placed on his theories by many educationists. In the words of Harold Rosen (1973), one of Bernstein's critics, 'whereas in the fifties children had their IQs branded on their forehead, in the sixties more and more of them had the brand changed to "restricted" or "elaborated".'

The incorporation of theories of cultural or linguistic deficit into programmes of intervention led to very discouraging results.

In the United States where most of the intensive work on deprived and disadvantaged children was carried out, it was found that out-of-school and pre-school programmes did not in the long term raise the intelligence or the achievement of the children involved. This result was in contradiction to the prevailing beliefs of the time. The most extreme statement of the faith in the environmental position was in the report of the experiment of Rosenthal and Jacobsen (1968), entitled *Pygmalion in the Classroom*. The findings of this experiment indicated that children are probably equal at birth, and that their ability is largely determined by the labels they acquire at home and at school. It was claimed that these will tend to have a 'self-fulfilling' effect. By the end of the 1960s, however, it became increasingly clear that the roots of educational failure went far deeper than the interpersonal relationships of the classroom, or the amount of cultural stimulation in the immediate environment.

The apparent failure of the intervention programmes (such as Operation Headstart) to produce permanent results in educational outcomes was brought home by the findings of large-scale investigations into the effects of school environments. The Coleman Report and the Plowden Report, both published in the mid-1960s, showed that for the US and Britain respectively, the major source of cognitive inequality was not located in schools – in their material resources, staff–student ratios, or the training of their teachers – but rather in the home. There would therefore be only marginal changes in the inequality of outcomes even if all children were given the same school environment. A massive reallocation of resources in favour of the disadvantaged would not appreciably affect the slope of class chances at school and university. These two reports were followed by several other studies in the English-speaking world which indicated that the superior educational attainment of rich children did not stem from the ability of their parents to buy them the most stimulating kinds of school environments, but from the advantages that they brought to the school. In conjunction with the apparent failure of the direct programmes of intervention, these studies constituted a devastating attack on the whole conceptual framework of the 'compensatory' model.

The discrediting of this model, linked perhaps to the difficulty of obtaining the resources which its programmes required, has been followed by the divisive tendencies within the inequality debate as new and revived explanations compete for space and attention. The post-war compromise based on a belief in the positive social effects of educational reform has been replaced by deep cynicism as to the validity in continuing with present policies. As I hope to show, their cynicism is unnecessary and stems out of the fallacies in the approaches to educational reform typified in all the five models presented earlier. For the time being, however, it may be enough to point out that the change from liberal to extremist explanation in the 1970s may have been predicted out of the way that the educational inequality debate has evolved over the past three decades.

Two of the more extreme responses have already been outlined at the beginning of this chapter – the 'meritocratic' and the 'radical'. The schools of thought within the latter have also been described, but would bear further elaboration. Ironically, perhaps, in the light of his influence on the 'compensatory' model, Basil Bernstein was one of the first to repudiate the false assumptions of liberal optimism of the early 1960s in an article entitled 'Education cannot compensate for society' (1970). In this he exposed the hidden, simplistic beliefs in the programmes that would eradicate the supposed educational and cognitive deficiencies of non-middle-class backgrounds. The assumptions of 'deficit' and 'deprivation' assume, according to him, a naive belief in the superiority of certain life styles. Bernstein here attempts to show that his own model of educability was really based on a 'class conflict' if not a Marxist model of social change and reproduction.

There are others who, in trying to avoid the slur of 'middle-class colonialism', go in the opposite direction. Instead of attempting to eliminate educational inequality by directly changing the class system, these would rather alter the stereotypes which middle-class educators categorize and treat children from 'different' backgrounds. These writers, who may be called 'cultural relativists', see the school as an oppressive force, falsely attempting to make all children alike and blaming them when they fail to change. Ironically, it is the theories of Bernstein which come in for a major assault, notably from those who claim that non-standard varieties of English are as effective at communicating elaborate and complicated arguments as are the standard ones (Labov, in Keddie, 1973). It is possible to bring about radical change, according to these theorists, by abandoning the whole ideological apparatus of the educational system as represented in the stratification of knowledge (e.g. the belief that Latin is 'better' than woodwork), the typing of pupils according to background and the rejection of non-standard forms of speech. In this way, they would claim, the oppressive, socially reproductive functions of the school would be undermined.

Genotype and 'luck'

It would be misleading, however, to conclude that the main response to the demise of liberal explanations has been radical. It would be closer to the mark if one viewed the radical response as rather peripheral and confined mainly to students in colleges of education and universities. At the level of popular debate, two other models have claimed most of the attention. Both may be seen to have grown out of the failure of the liberal reforms of the post-war welfare state. The first of these, the geneticist, began as nothing more than an explicit restatement of the evolutionary elements in the liberal theory of opportunity and ended as a rather narrowly based argument for the inherent cognitive inequality of ethnic and socio-economic groups. The second, associated with Christopher Jencks' *Inequality* (1972), called into question the empirical relevance of any of the liberal reforms and proposed that chance or 'luck' is as good an explanation as any of how the 'inequality machine' operates. I shall attempt to show that both Jencks' position and that of the geneticists are fundamentally misguided, both empirically and theoretically, in later chapters (particularly Chapter 5). Let us, however, look briefly at each in turn.

The opening sentence of Arthur Jensen's article in the winter edition of the Harvard Educational Review (1969) brilliantly caught the changing temper of the time: 'Compensatory education has been tried and it apparently has failed'. Jensen's long and scholarly article, controversial though it was, appears to be nothing more than a conservative statement of the premises of the 'evolutionary liberal' position, rather than a totally new approach to the differences in intellectual capacity. Jensen's main argument was, not as has been thought, that racial differences are genetically based, but that the innate capacity had been ignored during the 'compensatory' era and that is why programmes such as Operation Headstart were expecting too much.

At the time, of course, this was heresy, but it should be remembered that the claim that there may be a large genetic component in measured ability underlay the organization of secondary education with its appropriate 'tracks', or schools for children of different capacity. In the middle of the century it was held widely that innate capacity equips students for different types of secondary education, just as surely as it is held today by liberals and even by radicals that not everyone can be trained in a traditional university discipline. It should also be noted that the critics of post-war reforms have often used measures of intelligence to indicate the stability of the system of opportunity. Indeed, one well-known study in comprehensive schools (Ford, 1969) demonstrated that streaming was unfair because it favoured social class *rather* than measured ability. What was crucial to the public reaction to Jensen's statement was the implication that *group* and not just *individual* differences in educability could be explained genetically.

It may have been the sensitivity of liberal conscience at the time, it may have been the racial conflict in the United States, or it may have been the fact that ideological thinking was back in vogue, but the restatement of the evolutionary liberal position in 1969 was received as an inflammatory justification of social and racial inequality. Though the former liberal position was often based on a demonstration of the randomness of innate ability, the defenders of testing in the 1970s emphasized its *systematic* relationship to established forms of privilege, both racial and economic.

The possibility that the large 'gap' in the intelligence scores of blacks and whites in the United States would not be inconsistent with the genetic hypothesis was raised by Jensen. This remark, which was made in a relatively small section of the long 1969 article, was exaggerated out of all proportion by the popular reaction. Henceforth, the debate about the genetic component in intelligence was to be inseparable from the contentious issue of racial inequality. Jensen was labelled as a 'scientific racialist' and a large amount of publicity was given to his public performances and the attempts by student demonstrators to stop them. The debate was taken up by several proponents of the geneticist position, notably by H. J. Eysenck who experienced much the same difficulty in communicating with undergraduates in England as did Jensen in the United States. The most heated reactions, however, in the early 1970s greeted the appearances of Richard

Herrnstein who, more than any other writer, used the inheritance of ability as a defence for social and economic inequality at large.

Herrnstein's article *IQ* appeared in a national monthly in the United States, two years after Jensen's in the *Harvard Educational Review*. Herrnstein employed a syllogism which extrapolates the present tendencies towards selection by merit and the equalization of environments. This syllogism appeared (in a slightly amended form) in Herrnstein's book, *IQ in the Meritocracy* 1973: if differences in mental ability are inherited, if social success requires these abilities and if the environment is equalized, then to some extent social status will depend upon inherited differences. This syllogism is, as will be shown in Chapter 4, fraught with logical and empirical error. However, Herrnstein's case is interesting, not so much for the 'objective' validity of his conclusion that 'our society may be sorting itself willy-nilly into inherited castes', but for the theoretical shift that it denoted. The IQ test, which was originally an instrument of opportunity, had now become an excuse for inherited inequality, and the 'evolutionary liberal' position has merged with that of the extreme conservative.

The description of the changes within the 'inequality debate' over the past thirty years thus presents some interesting problems. First of all, the causal structure of educational inequality has never, it would appear, been adequately grasped because the terms of the debate are continually modified by the effects of policy. Since most of the policies have failed, we can only gain the impression that educationalists and sociologists are merely the passive respondents to the ebb and flow of public debate, and not, as it appeared at the beginning of this description, the authors of fresh and creative solutions. Each successive generation of writers has put forward a set of explanations usually within the terms of one of the five models presented at the start of the chapter, but has in every instance failed miserably to either command or even predict the course of events. One is led to conclude that *all* of the models may present over-simplified and indeed ideologically inspired pictures of the ways in which the six dimensions of educational inequality are causally related.

Jencks and after

This scepticism is aroused even further by the findings of Christopher Jencks and his associates (*Inequality*, 1972), who embarked towards the end of the 1960s on a work of social scientific detection which attempted to unravel all the causal processes of social mobility in America. This major enterprise was made possible by the existence of several ground-breaking studies which had already provided the data, and many of the techniques for such analysis. The most important of these was the work of Otis Dudley Duncan and his associates (1972). This was supplemented by the reports of the effects of school environments (notably those of Coleman and Plowden mentioned above) and by a host of studies on the acquisition of intelligence. The existence of this range of data covering the whole life cycle of post-war Americans provided an unprecedented opportunity for the observation and analysis of the causal structure of inequality as it was worked out in the lives of individuals.

The conclusions of Jencks are astounding. Not only are the liberal models that informed the policies of the post-war state shown to be ineffectual, but so too are those which claim that individual life chances are dominated by family background, IQ genotype or cognitive ability. Thus Jencks claims: that (1) the quality of the school environment is largely irrelevant to inequality in cognitive skills, credentials or life chances; (2) family background does not determine life chances, since there is almost as much income inequality among brothers as among men in general; (3) genetic advantage explains only a small proportion of differences in status and income, only about ten per cent of any cycle of inherited privilege; (4) if one compares men who are identical in family background, cognitive skill, educational *and* occupational attainment, one finds only 12 to 15 per cent less (income) inequality than among random individuals.

Jencks' study, therefore, shows the inadequacy of the five traditional approaches to the problem of defining and predicting the determinants of occupational and economic inequality. The huge amount of 'unexplained' variation in his model leads Jencks to propose that life chances are as much a matter of 'luck', personality, and on-the-job competence as anything else. He claims that one may as well ignore the attempt to restructure opportunity and concentrate on equalizing incomes directly, by 'insurance' schemes and the like.

Jencks' conclusions seem to be dismal and negative, but it is difficult to deny their empirical basis. The social engineering approach of the liberal welfare state has failed to make life chances more equal, since individuals are not apparently successful because of their superior cognitive abilities, educational achievements or 'better' backgrounds. Apparently, too, none of the reforms of this century has made American society more meritocratic, more egalitarian in its ladders of social ascent or much fairer in its reward structures. This would appear to be a strong indictment of social science as well as of the policy models that it has inspired.

One of the more common responses in England to Jencks' conclusions is that his findings are of purely American interest. England is ('as everyone knows') extremely class-ridden, with an educational system to fit. Therefore what Jencks (or any other sociologist) says about the American social structure does not apply to a system where only exceptional members of the working class rise socially, where 'cycles of deprivation' are apparently very strong and where the independent schools recruit only among the rich and powerful. The most enlightened policy, according to this response, is to continue with a policy of comprehensive reform, to abolish early selection in all its latent forms, and to reallocate money to poorer schools and neighbourhoods. This logic, as shall be shown later, is misguided, not simply because the forms of secondary schooling (Chapter 3) have little or nothing to do with the organization of educational opportunity, but also because the patterns of social mobility and of inequality in the US and Britain are strikingly similar. For these reasons it could be a mistake to continue with policies of social engineering in Britain (or indeed any industrialized country) that did not take into account the American experience.

Policy vs. theory

It would be wrong to think of Jencks, however, as a sociologist in the conventional sense, since he is more concerned with the applications of social science rather than with its theoretical basis. This may explain why so many who hold a 'class conflict' model tend to ignore him or treat his conclusions as somehow marginal to the main issues of social inequality. This may explain too why political and academic debate have grown so far apart in recent years with the former being dominated by extremely practical schemes (such as 'vouchers') while the latter has become increasingly critical and reflective. The post-Jencks era of the

1970s has been marked by a falling off in the free flow of ideas between those who write and those who make decisions.

The reason for the lack of communication between theorists and practitioners is not difficult to explain. In the first place theorists tend to see inequality as a set of relationships between large groups of people based on occupation, income or at a deeper level on their power and wealth. Education is then considered either justly or unjustly, as an instrument for reproducing and maintaining these relationships. On the other hand, social policy-makers are more concerned with individual biographies, with the distribution of people across these groupings and with the characteristics of ability, background and training that determine individual chances. In the latter case it is all too easy to forget about the 'structure of the maze' while in the former it is tempting to forget that sociology is about individuals and not just their group stereotypes. Jencks' study, more than any other, has exposed the fact that the policies of the welfare state must work at both levels and that what is a weakness in the one is also a weakness in the other.

It may then be understandable that many sociologists can avoid dealing with Jencks because he does not deal with the 'big picture'. This is not much help, however, if this picture is largely unable to cope with the experiences of individual children. It is small wonder that policy-makers lose patience with sociologists who tell them that inequality is rooted in their middle-class attitudes and ideologies, or that the only thing that will improve the educational chances of the poor is a political revolution. The problems of illiteracy, material and social deprivation cannot be solved by decree. In liberal-democratic society there are questions of justice and equity that must be remedied in the terms of the given situation. The fact that many of these problems are tractable by present resources and technologies may render a purely critical and philosophical perspective all the more suspect.

Because extreme solutions tend to be offered by theorists, one might conclude that there is no available explanation of the ways socio-economic relations are translated into life chances. On the one hand we appear to have the monolithic picture painted by the 'meritocrats' and the 'radicals'; on the other, the real world which is governed by 'luck' or by an arbitrarily defined on-the-job competence. Is there no way of bridging this gulf? If there were, would it be possible to formulate policies that took into account the randomness of the opportunity process but which at the same time tried to limit the biases that derive from the unequal relations of the classes? Is it possible to grasp the essentials of the 'maze' of opportunity and mobility other than by simply investigating the interests of its designers or by keeping a tally of those who happen to have solved it? It would appear that until sociologists have tried to answer these questions it will not be possible for policy-makers, parents and teachers to take them seriously.

Plan of the book

This book represents an attempt to do just this, by compiling the evidence against the simple interpretations of inequality offered by the five traditional models and by bringing together the most constructive theories and approaches to have emerged in the past five or six years. Such an attempt will lead us first to examine the theory of a 'tightening bond' between education and jobs that lies at the heart of liberal thinking on opportunity and national efficiency (Chapter 2). This will be followed in Chapter 3 by a detailed account of the hoped-for effects of equalizing the school environment, notably from the changeover from selective to comprehensive secondary schooling. In Chapter 4 we look at the 'great IQ debate' and see whether the failure of compensatory reform may be accounted for by group differences in inherited capacities. This leads into a full discussion in Chapter 5 of the mechanisms of social reproduction in the mobility process. As we shall see, it would be a mistake to conclude that Jencks' *Inequality* is the final word on the subject since there have appeared more recent interpretations which provide a more plausible explanation of the 'luck' of the privileged. These are the basis for the reformulation of policy in the traditions of the liberal reforms of the post-war years, but which employ a different approach (Chapter 6).

The contention of this book, then, is that the liberal theories of opportunity have not been falsely inspired but simply misdirected It is hoped that the reader will follow the arguments presented critically and will perhaps acquire a taste for further reading among the references provided. Finally, in view of the unfavourable economic climate of the present decade, it should be pointed out that reform is not always costly, and that a radical change of course may sometimes serve the interests of both efficiency and of social justice.

2

Education and jobs – the 'tightening bond' examined

The belief that there is a 'tightening bond' between education and jobs lies at the heart of the 'liberal' and 'meritocratic' models described in the first chapter, and has been the chief inspiration of the reforms of the post-war era. Simply, this belief is stated in the form of a proposition that as societies become more complex the old class divisions break down and merit, rather than birth, becomes the criterion of success. There will be, in other words, a tighter relationship observed between credentials and inequalities in pay, status and power. This thinking lay also behind the 'human capital' school of economic thought and has emerged in even newer form in the 'post-industrial' model of modern society.

One might expect, if this thesis were valid, that the relationship between credentials and, say, income, would have increased over this century in industrialized countries. After all, is it not much more difficult to get any kind of job without some form of school certificate, and do not the better jobs go to people who have been trained in universities and colleges? Put this way, the truth of the thesis seems self-evident, but on closer inspection it is, as we shall find out, very difficult to prove.

Let us look at the following case. John and Jim both go to

secondary school. John goes on to university and gets a high status job, but Jim drops out and ends up with a low status job. Both in the course of time encourage their own children to achieve and to stay on at school. When these children come to enter the job market, however, they may find that the credentials that they hold are not their only qualification. If we compared the power of extra schooling to 'buy' a better status job for both generations, we may find that because the general level of qualification has gone up, it is just as difficult to obtain an economically useful credential. Because of the 'push' from parents and the 'pull' from employers, schooling may have become a common commodity and its value inflated. It will appear, however, that the job market has become more meritocratic, but this could have been the simple result of a self-fulfilling prophecy. We should not be surprised if John's children find that their 'better' home background makes it easier for them to obtain a higher credential and to use it to obtain a higher status job.

The relationship observed between jobs and education may therefore be a good deal more difficult to untangle than it appears on the surface. It may be that the reader has already realized that the kinds of interpretations one can place on the relationship will stem from the models of inequality that were outlined in the previous chapter. The idea that credentials have little to do with merit on the job is, of course, a 'class conflict' approach. Education is just a form of status culture and credentials are a symbol of privileged background in this model. There may be more competition for credentials but this is artificially created by the employers, teachers and politicians in order to ensure that working-class children cannot rise too high.

It is on this issue that the 'class conflict' or 'radical' model, and the 'liberal' and 'meritocratic' models are in deep disagreement. This clash implies not just a simple description of the life cycle, but whole theories of productivity, employability and of social justice. It would be misleading, therefore, to limit the argument to a description of changes in the education of the workforce, a kind of manpower analysis. This has been the tendency in the sociology of education in the past and it has been the cause, as much as anything else, of the disillusionment with the policies of liberal reform.

Although we may start with 'the facts' in order to assess the strength of the bond, we will need to go beyond this to understand its nature. There are four basic questions in this area which we will look at in turn:

1 Is there a general educational upgrading of the workforce? If so, what is its distribution across the occupational hierarchy?
2 Is the possession of educational credentials becoming more important for success? (This is the essence of the 'tightening bond' thesis.)
3 What effect has the expansion of educational opportunity had on the extremes of privilege?
4 What is the basis of any observed relationship between educational credentials and life chances – does a credential really add to the productivity of labour or is it simply a device for selecting applicants by their social backgrounds?

1 Educational upgrading and its distribution

There is no doubt that the workforce of industrial nations is becoming better educated and that the distribution of credentials is becoming more equal. This was shown quite clearly in the data presented at an OECD conference on policies of educational expansion (1969b). In the General Household Survey (1973 : 245) of Britain, for example, it appears that 80 per cent of men aged 65 and over, as against only 43 per cent of men aged 20–4, held no qualifications. For the USA the average years of schooling for similar groups rises from about 8·5 to well over 12 (Beverly Duncan, 1968). This democratization of credentials must be seen in absolute terms for the moment. It merely indicates that the gap in the *number of years* that children of different abilities and backgrounds stay on in the school system has decreased. It does not tell us anything about the relationship between schooling and the other dimensions of inequality.

One may ask first how this upgrading was distributed over occupational categories. Do professionals as well as semi-skilled labourers have an equal number of years added on to their entrance requirements or is the distribution of this upgrading less even? One of the more interesting articles in this area comes from the research of Folger and Nam (1964) who carried out a painstaking study of the changing relationships between educational attainment and occupational structure for the United States. They show that during this century 85 per cent of the upgrading of jobs has occurred *within* the broad bands of status (professions, skilled trades and so on).

This conclusion finds support in a note of Halsey (1974) on the Nuffield Study of social mobility in Britain where it appears that a large part of the educational differentiation of the workforce is largely based on part-time and vocational training. The upgrading does not, therefore, fall along a single line of occupational status, but is distributed within a grid according both to general social status and to position achieved at the workface. This is a very important distinction since it implies that there may be really two systems of educational stratification rather than one, a finding which supports Giddens' (1973: 107) distinction between broad types of class 'structuration'. Although it is possible that both may be related they should not be confused when talking about a 'tightening bond'. If cab drivers were to organize into an exclusive profession for which an engineering degree was essential, they may be able to transform their status and earnings. They would still be offering much the same service, however. On the other hand, a diploma in advanced book-keeping may help an insurance executive to perform his job better but it does not assure his rise in the office hierarchy.

In some cases, however, the increased pressures towards educational upgrading within certain categories may be reflected in a tightening relationship at the workface. Halsey (1975b: 522), for example, points out although there has been a general rise in the educational threshold at 'virtually every point in the status hierarchy', this trend has been particularly marked in the middle ranges of technicians, supervisors and skilled manuals. How this 'patchiness' which he discerned in upgrading works itself through into a changing pattern of rewards is not clear, however. Although there may be incentives within firms and industries for higher levels of qualification, a detailed study of the tightening bond at the workface has yet to be carried out. Further evidence of the British case awaits the publication of a monograph by Goldthorpe and Llewellyn which will give a detailed description of the educational contours of the workforce. It should be pointed out that, despite the existence of tightening relationships between credentials and position, pay and 'perks' within some industries, particularly those where technological demand is greatest, the lines of status and power in the nation as a whole do not appear to have been significantly altered.

2 Education, life chances and structural change

The distribution of educational differentials in the labour force leads naturally to an examination of the association between credentials and life chances. One might suspect that the upgrading in formal education of the whole workforce would be a sign that a worker's qualifications would be a much better predictor of his life chances than they were, say, thirty years ago. Although as we have just seen the 'bond' works in complex ways, we might expect that there will have been some tightening as the whole workforce becomes middle class due to the elimination of low-skilled occupations. We might, therefore, predict a changing association alongside a structural shift towards higher skilled occupations whose entry is largely determined by credentials. Such a development is sure to produce some paradoxes. As we shall see, however, the final result may still be one of general stability. There are three main aspects to be examined here:

(*a*) the general structural changes of the workforce
(*b*) the size of the association between education, status and income
(*c*) the change in the association over this century.

(a) *Structural shifts in the workforce*

As with figures for educational upgrading, the structural changes in the workforce are indisputable. Over this century and particularly in the past thirty years the advanced economies have expanded the categories of non-manual and skilled groups and proportionately decreased the size of the unskilled sectors of the workforce. As Halsey (1975a) points out for Britain, the percentage of unskilled labour has fallen from 14·8 per cent in 1931 to 8·5 per cent in 1966, while the white-collar classes grew by 176 per cent between 1911 and 1966. Bell (1974: 17) shows that for the United States there has been a vast increase in the numbers of scientific and technical workers, who all require some form of tertiary education. Bell also notes that over the past decade or so the growth rate of the professional and technical class has been twice that of the average labour force, while that of scientists and engineers has been triple that of the working population. This illustrates the trend in the 1960s noted in Chapter 1, towards a huge investment in 'human' capital, as well as in sophisticated technology.

The growth in the service sector is particularly indicative. An OECD survey (1969a) showed that this sector now accounted for between 40 and 50 per cent of the labour force in western Europe. The United Kingdom has been particularly subject to this trend, with a growth of 32 per cent in the non-industrial sector over the years 1961–73, as against one of only 12 per cent for the US and 16·5 per cent for France (Eltis, 1975). Such a dramatic structural change has provided the empirical basis for the argument that the advanced economies are now entering a 'post-industrial' era. In this society it is held that knowledge will be more important than capital and that technical competence will determine the power relationships of social groups. The analysis of manpower requirements should not, however, be taken as necessary evidence of a new form of inequality, since they may simply disguise the old forms.

(b) *The size of the credentials–life chances correlation*

Despite the historical coincidence of the 'embourgoisement' of the workforce and the greater equality in the schooling of different occupational groups, it does not appear that the relationship between credentials and either income or status has 'tightened' significantly. This does not mean that it is unwise to obtain a higher level of qualification, it simply means that the *relative* rewards have not increased, a point we shall return to later.

There are, of course, appreciable personal benefits to be gained from more schooling. Education exerts a sizeable effect on lifetime earnings in nearly every country (Psacharopoulos, 1972). For each additional year of schooling there is about a ten per cent return on investment, with a slightly higher rate for college or university education. A census study (1968) in the US for example showed that males who had no high school education earned only 85 per cent of the average national income, as against 170 per cent for college graduates. For female workers the income was lower and the slope of the differential more gradual, rising from 47 per cent to 84 per cent of the average income for each of these educational groupings.

Let us look at the British case in more detail. The General Household Survey (1973 based on 1971 data) showed that 44 per cent of male graduates earned more than £3,000 p.a. while only

1·7 per cent of males holding no qualifications earned this much. Since 1971 there appears to have been a good deal of erosion of such differentials in the UK owing to inflation and government income policies. However, there is good evidence (*Sunday Times*, 3 August 1975, p. 38) that the take-home pay of top status positions (for which graduate entry is often an advantage) is still two or three times as great as that of the middle groups. The extra benefit of completing a degree is quite dramatic for males. For female workers it is the simple fact of having some higher education that appears to yield the greatest returns. A female worker (GHS, 1973) with some higher education had a 50 per cent chance of earning between £1,250 and £1,500 p.a. as against only a 7·5 per cent chance for her co-worker with only GCE qualifications ('A' or 'O' levels).

Impressive as these figures may sound, it is still possible to find a good deal of discrepancy between education and earnings if we look at individuals rather than at group averages. So much unpredictability is there in this association that one might question the neat proposition that inequalities in rewards are in line with structure of demands for skilled performance. The relationship may be high at the upper end of the educational spectrum as just noted, but in the middle and at the bottom of the scale there is a good deal of indeterminacy. Crowder (1974) notes that for the relationship between education and income in the US 'the most salient observable pattern is that of the approximately normal distribution of income within each educational category with moderately rising mean incomes with increasing educational attainment levels'.

In Britain too the picture between the extremes and sometimes even at the bottom end is very confused. Referring again to the General Household Survey (1973) it would appear that the percentage of males earning at or above the middle range (£1,250–£1,500) is only loosely related to their educational level. At the 'degree or equivalent' level 93 per cent of males were earning in the upper half of the income range, while in the 'below degree higher education' level there were 89·7 per cent; for holders of GCE 'A' levels 67·6 per cent, for 'O' level holders 59·2 per cent; for CSE holders 57·7 per cent and for males without formal qualifications 46·4 per cent. Similarly for females the economic advantages of extra schooling, outside higher education, are often unclear. For female workers the midmost income for those holding 'A' and 'O' levels was slightly *below* that for those with CSE or other qualifications.

Despite the fact that socio-economic scales incorporate a degree of educational bias, the association between credentials and status is similarly imperfect. As Halsey (1975b) shows from the recent data of the Nuffield study, one could hardly suppose that the meritocracy was just around the corner since 'even the higher grade self-employed or salaried professionals, who have the highest social standing, have at most a quarter of their members with university degrees'. In most of the middle categories, only a 'tiny minority' of graduates appear, and all those below are largely non-graduate. Similarly, Crowder (1974:28) notes that for the US there is a wide range of socio-economic status within the three largest attainment categories, with 22 per cent of high school graduates climbing into the upper status groups. Surely the liberal assumptions of educational stratification do not lead us to predict such a degree of 'slippage'. It appears that education may ration the chances of obtaining the higher levels of status and income but it by no means guarantees it. We must conclude, then, that the 'tightening bond' thesis is far from vindicated – even in such a crude analysis as this.

(c) *Changes in the correlation of credentials and life chances*

It is, of course, the changing or dynamic aspects of the correlation by which the 'tightening bond' is to be tested, and not simply by its apparent 'looseness' at any point in time. If allowances are made for the fact that education has a slightly greater value for those just coming into the labour force (i.e. younger men), the relationship between credentials and life chances has apparently changed very little over this century. This in one way bears out the conclusions of Folger and Nam that the demand for skills in broad status categories has been relatively constant. Jencks (1972:327), for example, remarks that the correlation between education and occupation has shown no increase in the US since 1900. The correlation between education and earnings shows some variation in the US (Duncan *et al.*, 1972:38) but hovers at about the same size for four broad age groups. There is no comparable data for changes in earnings and education in British literature, but the relationship between education and occupational status does not appear to be demonstrably higher for younger men (Halsey, 1975b:524). The fact that the relationship between education and rewards has held steady under the spread of mass secondary and tertiary education points to a paradox at the heart of the 'tightening bond' that needs to be explained.

The paradox of rising educational levels

We have seen from the first two sub-sections of this chapter that (1) there has been an overall upgrading of the educational qualifications of the workforce over the past half-century in two industrialized countries, (2) that there has been a structural shift in the workforce towards jobs that demand a higher educational qualification for entry. Nevertheless, as we have just seen, there has been no 'tightening' of the association between educational qualifications and individual rewards. Life chances may be more dependent on a certain level of qualification in an absolute sense (i.e. having a secondary school certificate as against holding no qualification), but in a relative sense, the new level of qualification appears to 'buy' the same amount of status and income as the old.

This tendency towards the inflation of credentials is often obscured, however, in the span of a single generation. It may *appear* that schooling will bring in more benefits at one time than another, but this is to be balanced with the fact that the affluence of the whole population has been rising at the same time as the general level of education.

It may be useful to think of this paradox in terms of the following analogy. Imagine a busy escalator in a department store. There are several people lining up to use it and it is quite crowded on the machine itself. It makes a good deal of sense for most people to use the escalator because it is quicker and more direct than the stairway and in any case takes a lot less effort. Some passengers jostle to the front of the line and a few actually walk or run up the moving stairs, but in general, the movement up and down is closely related to the time each person joined the line and stepped onto the machine. If we think of the educational system as a kind of 'escalator' of life chances which moves everybody up but preserves the differential in an original order, the paradox may, therefore, be easier to understand. We may be able to perceive too why educational expansion may be popular and at the same time relatively powerless to change the original inequalities between its 'passengers'.

3 The equalization of social rewards

One might expect as a test of the 'tightening bond' thesis to see certain structural changes taking place in the distribution of rewards as educational qualifications become more accessible and consequently more evenly spread among the population. Such a test could help us to probe specific aspects of the thesis and serve as well to link this descriptive section to the next where we look at the theoretical basis of the correlation between education and life chances. If it can be shown that the distribution of certain important rewards is stable, despite the structural and educational changes of the century, there may be some reason for suspecting that the 'bond' is not the outcome of economic or technical pressures at all, but rather of deep-seated tendencies in the social system to allocate rewards on the non-meritocratic and ascriptive basis of family background.

We could, therefore, find some support for the 'class conflict' model which points to the enduring inequalities of industrial society and explains these in terms of the unequal distribution of economic power rather than of technical knowledge. We will examine three areas of social stratification – élite mobility, the over-time correlation between fathers' and sons' occupational status, and the changing share of the national income of lower income groups. If the 'tightening bond' were working in the direction indicated by the models examined, we might therefore expect that:

(*a*) access to élite groups is becoming more meritocratic
(*b*) the correlation between fathers' and sons' occupational status is decreasing
(*c*) that the percentage of the national income of the lower paid is increasing.

(a) *The membership of élite groups*

A salient feature of the membership of élites in western societies is that it tends to be hereditary. This may not of course be surprising to someone holding a 'radical' or a 'traditional élitist' model, but the permanence of this tendency bears comment. Even though such groups represent only a tiny proportion of the population, their membership is of enormous importance for judging the political effects of educational expansion.

For the USA and the UK there is a good deal of evidence that the membership of top decision-making groups in the nation is drawn from families of similar class background. A recent study of the educational background of British élites by David Boyd (1973), for example, found that the public school/Oxbridge route to élite status may have strengthened rather than weakened since the 1930s and that the inheritance of status between those who have entries in *Who's Who* is still quite pronounced. Again, Halsey and Crewe (1967) showed that recruitment to the administrative class of the civil service in Britain had actually become more restrictive in terms of public school and Oxbridge education than it was before the second world war. In this connection Kelsall's (1957) study of Cambridge undergraduates revealed that only a very small proportion were from working-class origins. Collins (1971) argues, with a good deal of evidence, that a similarly narrow route to élite recruitment – private prep. school, Ivy League college and prestigious professional school – is still quite dominant in the United States. In France, the strength of upper middle-class background for entry to the 'grandes écoles' has persisted despite numerous post-war reforms (Bourdieu and Saint-Martin, 1974).

It is not difficult to draw the conclusion that, despite the expansion of educational opportunity created in the post-war period, self-recruitment to élite decision-making groups through education – in the civil service, in business and in national institutions – has not increased dramatically. One might even conclude that the points of entry to the privileged educational routes and from these routes into the 'top' positions has in fact narrowed according to their social base. There may have been vacancies created by expansion of scientific and technological professions, but it should be remembered that this has occurred mainly at a sub-élite level. On the whole the educational upgrading of the post-war period does not appear to have changed recruitment patterns to the most strategically placed groups. Although this is evidence for the 'class conflict' model, it does not alter the fact that a great deal of mobility does take place and that the chances of social demotion for 'élite' children have always been quite high.

(b) *The inheritance of status*

Another prominent feature of stratification systems is that the correlation between fathers' and sons' occupational status has remained fairly stable from decade to decade. The extent of inequality of social opportunity, therefore, appears to be unaffected by both educational and demographic movements. This is made even more remarkable by the fact that, despite the differences in the economic conditions that may affect mobility, such as rapid industrialization, the size of correlation in different countries is very similar. Svalastoga (1965) summarizing the findings of mobility studies for nine European countries found that the likelihood of predicting a son's occupational status from that of his father was not appreciably greater in one country than in another. The relationship for the United States is only slightly weaker than for these and, like the others, remarkably stable. In fact the correlation for men aged 24–34 in the US is almost identical with that of the 55–65 cohort (Duncan *et al.*, 1972: 38). For Britain the stability of this correlation over three generations is equally apparent from Ridge's (1974: 63–4) analysis of data from the earlier Glass study (1954).

We may conclude then from this discussion that the factors that may be decreasing educational inequality are probably not the same as those that are affecting social inequality. Contrary to the expectations of a 'tightening bond' the influence of family background on sons' educational placement appears not to be diminishing. We have not looked at the 'geneticist' possibility that the class distribution of intelligence may be the cause of this stability. However, as we shall see in the Appendix to Chapter 4, this argument is not particularly convincing since the inheritance of status is only fractionally attributable to inherited ability. Since social background appears to be exerting a constant influence on social achievement, we might conclude that there are non-meritocratic forces at work in the selection process which are intransigent to the kinds of social engineering envisaged by educational reformers.

(c) *Educational inequality and income redistribution*

We turn finally to the third prediction from the 'tightening bond' thesis, the expected redistribution of income that attends the equalization of formal attainment. Since raising the school leaving age has by definition a marked affect on the average formal attainment of a cohort, representing a huge social investment, we might predict, following the liberal credo, that a greater equality of income might result.

In fact, the opposite appears to be the case. A good test of this hypothesis is in the changing share of the national income of the lower paid. Lester Thurow (1972) carried out such an investigation for the United States. His comparison of the income gap between the top and the bottom fifths of the income distribution for the period 1950–70 showed that their respective shares of the national income became slightly more unequal despite the decreasing gap in years of full-time education. The same result appears from an analysis of the black/white income differential. From 1952 to 1968 the mean educational attainment of black workers rose from 67 per cent to 87 per cent of that of their white counterparts, but their median incomes rose by only 8 per cent – from 58 to 66 per cent.

In the UK there appears to be a parallel to the Thurow finding. Frank Field (1974) quotes from British Labour Statistics (1971) and Hansard (1974) to show that over the past ninety years the relative position of the poorest tenth of male manual workers has not improved. In 1886 they earned 68·6 per cent of the average male manual earnings, in 1973 67·3 per cent. Despite the large gains by the poor in terms of formal education since 1944 the effect on their relative share of the national income is not apparent. Notwithstanding some of the tendencies towards income equalization noted by the Diamond Commission Report (1975) and in the recent effects of inflation and government pay policies, this bottom group is still no better off. This is graphically shown by recent studies of the effects of inflation on the lower paid in Britain (Willmott, 1976).

It is therefore very difficult to maintain that the returns on extra years of education for children of the poor is one means of decreasing income inequality as measured by annual earnings. If the whole population is better educated, it does not follow that the poorest are necessarily able to convert their new found opportunity to economic advantage. This evidence may explain the cynicism of low achievers towards the benefits of extra schooling, particularly when this is imposed by legal sanctions. Despite the increasing bias in the labour market towards qualified school leavers, the lot of those who are at the bottom of the queue is not demonstrably better.

When viewed from an individual, rather than an historical and group perspective, the advantages of extra schooling for low achievers would also appear to be quite negligible. The earnings of workers with no qualifications, both male and female, in Britain (General Household Survey, 1973: figure 7.3) are not appreciably different for those with CSE grades 2–5; indeed, up to a certain point they even tend to be better. For Britain, as Jencks (1972: 224) claims for the US, it appears that 'efforts to get everyone to finish high school and attend college must be justified primarily on non-economic grounds'.

If there is a 'cycle of inequality', as Field claims, then this surely is a point at which it is most inequitable. More affluent, higher achieving students are better able to exploit the educational system in order to increase the distance between themselves and their less advantaged fellows. The disabling effects of a poorer background and its educational handicaps multiply the costs and diminish the benefits of the extra year of formal schooling. We shall turn to this problem again in Chapter 6 and examine how such a tendency can be altered. What *is* certain is the inefficacy of conventional approaches to equalizing provision, since these if anything have provided a subsidy to those who are both educationally and socially privileged.

In conclusion then, the three tests of the 'tightening bond' appear to yield unsatisfying results. The supposed effects of educational reform in an increasingly technological society have not come to pass. There has been little change in the social composition of élites in the extent of social mobility or in the income share of the lower paid. Despite all this, employers hire increasingly according to credentials and educational background, and politicians claim that educational expansion can be a great social leveller. Above all, there is the enduring optimism, now somewhat faded perhaps, that educational spending will be good for the economy, will decrease poverty and will open up the highest echelons in the land to the children of the lowliest origins. Even more than this, the hopes of educational reformers have often been linked to a particular form of secondary schooling. There are probably deep-seated folk beliefs in these tenets of educational expansion and innovation. However, it is their justification in social and economic theory that is more interesting and to which we now turn as we attempt to answer the fourth question posed at the beginning of this chapter.

4 Theoretical interpretations of educational stratification

The connections that reformers have made between educational expansion and social progress are not new, but have been central to liberal thinking since the Enlightenment. The 'post-industrial' society is merely an extension of this long tradition. In the words of the chief exponent of this model, Daniel Bell (1974: 41), 'The post-industrial society, in dimension of its status and power, is the logical extension of this meritocracy; it is the codification of a new social order based, in principle, on the priority of educated talent'. Not too far from the social aspects of this model is the economic theory associated with the 'human capital' school of Theodore Schultz, Gary Becker and others, which as we saw earlier, sees investment in human beings as the basis for a revolution in economic thinking and social planning. One of the main foundations of this theory is the abundant evidence of the 'rates of return' on additional schooling.

The thinking underlying this approach informed a good deal of the social reform in the 1960s, particularly in the United States, where the newly 'discovered' poverty appeared to be amenable to educational remedies. The 'human capital' argument had two aspects. First, it was held that education is a form of national investment since it creates social as well as individual wealth, adds to the store of the nation's skills and provides the human basis for a modern economy. Second, educational investment was supposed to bring about an upsurge in individual life chances, and could, therefore, be deployed in the war against poverty, crime and technological unemployability. Delinquency, dropping out of school and personal failure were inextricably linked. The sociology of inequality had now found a liberal solution based on apparently sound economic reasoning. The old 'class conflict' models which saw education as a kind of useless status culture had apparently been outdated.

How precisely was education to achieve all this? The mechanism has been explained by Thurow (1972) in terms of an opposition between what he calls a 'wage competition' and a 'job competition' model. The former proposes that any increase in the educational level of low income workers will have three positive effects: (1) it will raise their productivity and consequently their earnings; (2) it will increase the supply of high-skill workers and consequently lower their wages; (3) it will create a shortage of low-skill workers and thus raise *their* wages. Thurow concludes that 'the net result is that as total output rises the distribution of earnings becomes more equal, and each individual is rewarded according to his merit. What could be more ideal?'

The beneficial effects predicted from this model have not come to pass, particularly, as we saw, in the most crucial aspect of increasing the income share of the lower paid. There are several reasons for suspecting that the correlation between education and earnings is a spurious one – that is, it tells us little more than that educated workers are paid more because employers like them, not because they are more productive. At several levels the evidence appears to favour this interpretation, though the issue is, as we shall see, slightly more complicated. We will look first at some of the evidence on productivity and then move on to a theoretical discussion.

It appears that the relationship between levels of education and productivity, whether we look at economic divisions, firms or at individual workers, is by no means pronounced. To begin with economic divisions, an OECD study which compared entire sectors of the economy across 52 countries revealed no clear relationship between the proportions of the labour force with different amounts of schooling and output per capita. The results of this study are disturbing, though as Blaug (1971:68) suggests, many other factors, such as natural resources, quality of management and work habits would need to be better controlled. However, at the level of the firm, the results of a cross-sectional study of the productivity and the educational structure of 68 plants in the British electrical engineering industry are distinctly negative (Layard *et al.*, 1971). There was no evidence that those plants with the highest proportions of educated personnel enjoyed (on a unit basis) higher rates of profit, larger sales, higher output or lower costs.

Finally, at the level of the individual worker, the evidence given by Ivar Berg (1970) would suggest that there may be a slightly *negative* relationship between physical productivity and educational qualifications. Berg's study would indicate that firms do not, in general, even bother to keep a record of the effectiveness of employees hired at different educational levels, even though they placed a good deal of emphasis on the possession of credentials at the time of hiring. An unqualified case for the 'wage competition' model, where jobs are chasing people with the necessary skills, where there is the 'invisible hand' of supply and demand to regulate the distribution of rewards, is difficult to sustain in the light of this evidence. Since workers are apparently hired on a number of characteristics not directly connected with their ability to 'deliver the goods', one is led to consider models that incorporate other mechanisms of selection.

Explanations of credentialism

The simplest alternative is what Blaug (1971) calls the 'psychological' explanation and what Thurow calls the 'job competition' model. These account for the correlation between earnings and education in terms of the purely symbolic value of credentials – they indicate a host of other characteristics desired by employers. Such characteristics – poise, docility, a charming manner or a desirable accent – add nothing to the marginal productivity of labour. Because of this, Blaug argues that we would have to conclude that educated employees exploit their less educated workmates. Thurow, in turn, can see little economic justification for the pursuit of credentials other than a purely competitive one: 'In effect', he claims, 'education becomes a defensive necessity to protect one's "market share".'

This 'psychological' explanation with the corresponding dynamic of 'job competition' where a credential merely guarantees a better place on the labour queue, may appear to be a little superficial since it postulates no links between schooling, the class structure or the relations of work. It does not explain *why* certain attributes are chosen and maintained in selection and hiring policies even if it eliminates those based on economics. For this reason we turn to consider what Blaug calls the 'sociological' explanation which has been more fully elaborated by Bowles and Gintis (1976). In this explanation, it is held that the real function of credentials is to facilitate the control and surveillance of capitalist enterprise. People with the 'right' educational backgrounds are better able to command and their higher levels of training may be used to legitimate the hierarchical division of labour.

Neither the 'psychological' nor the 'sociological' model can be accepted as they stand, however. The mere fact that education – be it in terms of cognitive skills, or personal characteristics – 'makes a difference' cannot be without *some* positive economic implications. While a Marxist may argue that these are mainly to do with the expropriation of the 'surplus value' produced by the workers, it is difficult to imagine a large organization where some degree of domination (as distinct from technical coordination) was not necessary (in this connection see Engels' *On Authority*, 1913–14). Moreover, in an age where technological innovation is closely linked with efficiency, it appears to be quite rational to hire educated workers not because of their specific skills, but because of the ease with which they can be re-trained.

It is necessary then to hold some kind of a balance between the models of educational stratification that emphasize respectively economic, psychological or sociological explanations. As Blaug suggests, all three may be true simultaneously. It may be suggested here that the 'economic' explanation is most applicable at times of high technological demand in which there is a good deal of competition among employers for scarce skills in the labour market, the 'psychological' explanation when there is a slackening of demand for specific skills, together with a high supply of 'over-educated' applicants. The 'sociological' explanation may be most appropriate when there is a threat to the legitimacy of the firm and a consequent need to reassert control by the demonstration of the technical or professional skill of managerial groups.

Conclusion

We appear to have come a long way from the 'tightening bond' thesis with its simple model of educational stratification and its hopes of greater social opportunity. The intimate functional relationship that it proposed between education and jobs is considerably complicated by the intransigence of the reward structure in the face of increasing educational equality and structural mobility. The economic basis of this relationship now appears to be naive – an extrapolation of the personal returns on educational investment and of the visible effects of education on 'getting ahead' at any point in time. As we have seen, neither at the very top of the social pyramid, nor at the very bottom, has the 'tightening bond' much application. In the middle the picture is quite confused and must always be offset against the structural changes in the labour force and the increased affluence of post-war society. For these reasons there is no evidence that the bond, weak and variable as it has been, is becoming tighter.

In summary, the relationship between education and jobs should, before any interpretation, be broken down into two interlocking structures. On the one hand, we have the formal educational system which feeds into the general social hierarchies of power, prestige and income. This mechanism certifies young people in general skills which enable them to compete for positions at various levels of occupational entry. On the other, we have the 'real world' of the work place in which these general skills are supposed to yield concrete results in the more efficient disposition of manpower. The connection between these two levels of stratification is very complex and cannot be summed up in a single proposition. The best we can do for the moment is to say that while there is some evidence of an increased tightening at certain points *within* occupational groups, there is overall a very stable pattern of educational opportunity and social ascent. The simplistic thinking that leads to expectations of rapid social reform through education are probably quite unfounded and, as Jencks demonstrates, all too easily shot down.

3

The school environment: does it matter?

One of the slogans that is attributed to the study of Jencks and which seeped into the mass media and staff rooms was the phrase 'schools make no difference'. What was meant was not that society should be 'deschooled' (that was a competing message at this time) but that the quality of the school environment does not make a great deal of difference to a person's life chances. The implications of this phrase are three-fold. First, it implies that the quality of the school has not a large effect on the achievement as measured by scores on standardized tests; secondly, that it does not affect the opportunity to acquire credentials; thirdly, that the quality of schooling does not affect life chances.

If all these statements were true, it follows that giving every child the same kind of school environment would not do very much to reduce inequality in social or educational outcomes. Most of the determinants of these outcomes would then reside in the environment outside the school or in the talents which the child himself brings to education. In the words of Alan Little (1971) whose argument along these lines predates Jencks, 'you may tell a Balliol man anywhere; but this is not so much the influence of Balliol as what was necessary to get, and stay, there'.

In this chapter, then, we move back from the credentials–jobs link and look at the effects of the differences in quality, rather than in the duration, of schooling. A good deal of the argument will be centred around the differences between comprehensive and selective school systems, since these represent opposed forms of rationing school environments and of opportunities for higher education.

In the following analysis we will look at the question of the rationing of school environments according to region, class and ability. We will then look in turn at the effects of the school environment on scholastic achievement, credentials and finally on life chances.

1 Rationing school environments

School quality may be defined as those aspects of the formal educational environment amenable to change by public or professional policy. This includes the physical nature of the school buildings, the type of equipment and facilities the school offers, the training, specialization and experience of its staff, the average per-pupil expenditure and the average size of class groups and the social and intellectual 'mix' of the pupils as a body. We might also include under 'policy' the ideological climate of the school or school district, teacher attitudes, types of control and 'compliance' and so forth. It is important to add in here the type of curriculum to which the student is exposed, since this rations a good deal of the opportunity to go on to higher study. Obviously here we are not using the term 'environment' in quite the same sense as before. The restriction of opportunity to take certain exams or to undertake certain courses necessary for college or university entrance is mainly a bureaucratic, not a material, constraint. Nevertheless, it must be included since it is possible, as we shall see later, to compare the effectiveness of different selection systems in extending opportunity to children of different abilities and backgrounds. Exposure to certain curricula thus represents an important dimension of the school environment.

The distribution of resources

The inequalities within countries in material educational provision are well documented. Moynihan (1972) describes a pattern for the US which he claims is typical – 'suburbs spend above the average, central cities at or slightly below the average, small towns and rural areas below the average'. Between states one finds glaring inequalities such as that between New York State which in 1970 had a per pupil expenditure of $1,237 as against $438 for Alabama. The difference between social classes and between suburbs and inner ring areas does not, however, appear to be very great, particularly in a comprehensive system. This was the finding of the Coleman report mentioned earlier where it appeared that the educational disadvantage of blacks in the US arose from the fact that so many lived in southern states rather than in urban 'ghettos'. Similarly, studies of the comprehensive schools of Britain indicate that a good deal of resources are often spent at the 'bottom end' of the ability range (Ross *et al.*, 1972). It also appears, in contradiction to conventional belief, that in comprehensive systems smaller classes, more stable teachers and a higher per-pupil expenditure may be more common in schools with a higher working-class intake (King, 1974).

Variations in materials and resources between *schools* in a selective system are another matter, of course. One dramatic finding in this regard was that of the Newsom Report (1963) which in a survey of secondary modern schools (where average or below average pupils are taught) showed that 80 per cent were more or less 'seriously deficient'. In addition, the findings of the Public Schools Commission (1968) noted the high material endowments of the independent sector as against that of the state sector. The combination of these findings with those cited in the previous paragraph might lead one to suspect that the case for comprehensive education was irrefutable from egalitarian premises. Certainly, the visible equality that a radical policy of comprehensivization brings about is hard to deny, but it may be misleading, as we shall see, to conclude that outcomes would be similarly equalized. Before we examine outcomes, however, let us look at the mechanisms of this 'rationing' in more detail.

Educational opportunity and school quality

A more important question for the rationing of school quality than its distribution across districts and types of system is its availability to children of different backgrounds and abilities.

What are the chances of a child from a certain family background and with a certain ability being in a school with better resources, more privileged class mates and a more intellectually challenging curriculum? This is, of course, an enormous question and the answers are not always easy to find. Generally, however, there is a relationship between high status background, high intelligence and all of these dimensions of the school environment.

The extent to which the school environment is rationed according to privilege and ability varies according to the type of inequality one is studying. On the expenditure side the differences are not too great. Jencks, for example, estimates that the differences in per-pupil expenditure is only \$6·50 per annum for families whose incomes differ by every \$1,000. For Britain, as we see above, the overlapping of the dimensions of school quality with selection makes a detailed analysis difficult. The correlation between social background and ability also complicates the pattern of opportunity, making a simple statement about the selective process fairly difficult. Certainly, in crude terms, there has been a lessening in the inequality of access to selective schooling since the war. Halsey (1975b: 519) notes that: 'What has happened is that whereas in the 1949 population a man who started life in a professional family had fifteen times as high a chance of selective secondary schooling as the son of a labourer, the differential had been reduced by 1972 to a factor of 6.'

How great are the influences of background as against those of ability in the post-war competition for grammar school places? There can be little doubt that the influence of ability is much greater than that of father's status, even if we ignore the tendency of brighter children to come from middle-class homes. The effect of ability is in fact about twice that of socio-economic status, when each is taken independently. It should be remembered, however, that socio-economic status is only a very rough index to the full range of advantages supplied by the home. These are, of course, not the same as socio-economic status (or social class, if one takes a different definition of inequality) but tend to be correlated with it (see Chapter 5). The danger here, as Davies and Bernstein (1969) point out, is that one could reduce social background to a set of family characteristics and obscure the hidden dimensions of power and wealth that unite them (see the discussion on social background in Chapter 5).

A comparison of the English selection system with the American 'track' system would seem to be useful here. This could be of wider sociological interest since a sociologist (Ralph Turner, 1960) has proposed two models of mobility through education that are typified by England and the United States respectively. The English system, according to Turner, is organized like a club, where the children are selected early in their careers and 'sponsored' by other members of the club. In the American system, however, the selection is carried out by means of a 'contest' where children are in constant competition right through their school careers. Turner made the rather surprising suggestion that comparative studies would show the English system to be fairer or more meritocratic than the American, in the sense of promoting ability rather than social background.

Until recently there has been no evidence to confirm or refute Turner's suggestion. An article by Kerckhoff (1974), however, examines not only the effects of ability and social background on attainment and credentials but on school selection and curriculum assignment as well. We shall look at the comparison of opportunity to obtain credentials later in this chapter. However, as to the latter problem, there does not seem to be very much advantage in either system. Kerckhoff concludes: 'Although the English boys were assigned to a school type at an early age (eleven or twelve) and the American boys chose a programme at a later stage (fifteen or sixteen) the division in the two countries almost identically reflects the contributions of ability and social origin.'

Although selection to a grammar school, or placement on a 'college track' does not constitute the full meaning of the term 'school environment' there is no doubt that it represents a major dimension of opportunity. We might doubt, therefore, if the American experience were any guide, whether 'going comprehensive' would really decrease the class bias in educational progress, or whether it would simply postpone it. We will return to this point later when we examine the educational and social effects of school quality.

2 How does the quality of schooling affect scholastic achievement?

Achievement means here scores on standardized tests such as those of vocabulary, reading, arithmetic and general knowledge, rather than place in class or school grades. These scores tend to correlate very highly with tests of intelligence and some sociologists (Coleman and Jencks) prefer not to make the distinction between them. In this section we are asking what effects a certain school environment will have on the skills that tests measure. Will it be found that there is a good deal of discrepancy between the scores of children who go to 'better schools' when social background is controlled for? This is an important question both for teaching and for public policy because it is often believed that the fact that poor children tend to have a worse school environment is the reason for their lower achievement, higher rates of illiteracy and so forth. It is often claimed that if only more money were provided in the schools for smaller classes and more qualified teachers, then the gap in the reading age between privileged and under-privileged children would be significantly reduced.

The evidence available from British and American studies is not encouraging to people who hold this 'compensatory' model of achievement. Differences between schools and between classrooms in environmental variables such as teacher/pupil ratios, teaching methods, facilities and ancilliary services, streamed versus non-streamed grouping, apparently have only marginal effects. In the first place the concept of 'bad school' is a very misleading one. There is a good deal of overlap between schools on their average measures of achievement. As Jencks (1972:91) claims for the US: 'eliminating differences between elementary schools would reduce cognitive inequality by 3 per cent or less'. The differences between high schools was found to be smaller. These findings are also very consistent with those of English studies, particularly those of the Plowden Report (Peaker, 1967; 1971).

In the second place, the search for the variable that makes one school better than another appears to be not very rewarding. The differences in per-pupil expenditure are the least important and the differences in any specific resource such as library books, smaller teacher/pupil ratios have only tiny effects. Higher teacher salaries have no appreciable effect either. In fact, the things that teachers, researchers and parents have always believed to be important aspects of school environment are not very significant after all when it comes to explaining the inequalities in children's cognitive abilities.

It is arguable, of course, that these test scores are not valid criteria of cognitive growth. It may be said that they measure only very narrow skills and that they do this very poorly. It is curious though that those who argue in this way against the validity of such tests, often to defend the superior habits of 'the mind' nurtured by traditional environments, are also those who wish to keep selective tests such as the 11+ when such institutions are threatened. It is difficult to claim that the cognitive skills measured by such tests are not important for survival in modern life, even though they may not be, as Jencks shows, a large component of economic success.

A culinary analogy, though a little bizarre, may be to the point. One may compare the nutritional effects of food with the pleasure it affords and find that there may be very little correlation. The nutritional effects of say British and French cooking may be identical, but the enjoyment often does not bear comparison. How might one compare, for example, 'sole bonne femme' with fish fingers? If one cannot estimate their relative subjective advantages with any accuracy, one can at least ascertain their ability to sustain life. Similarly, one can define and measure within reasonable limits the kinds of cognitive performances important for achievement at various levels of bureaucratic society. The fact that these may not be affected very much by the quality of the school should be central to any debate about equalizing the outcomes of education.

One cynic proposes that all this suggests that school reform should now be compared with rearranging furniture on board the *Titanic*. This is a rather extreme position but it is true that most of the claims for the beneficial effects of school reforms have fallen far short of the hopes of the early 1960s. It would be wrong to conclude that things will keep on going as they have been, and that there will be no sudden breakthrough in the manipulation of cognitive inequality through school policies. However, the prospect does not now look very bright, particularly when we consider the research on the specific methods of educational treatment within schools. The most thorough survey of existing research into these effects was carried out by the Rand Corporation in the early 1970s in a special report to the President's Commission (Averch, 1972). It concludes: 'the research on teaching approaches, teacher difference, class size and the like shows no consistent effect on student achievement as measured by standardized cognitive tests'. It appears that the search for the 'key' to cognitive inequality is much more difficult than in the 1960s when it appeared that educational technology and innovative methods were to revolutionize learning.

The social 'mix' and achievement

If all the effects of between school differences are isolated, it appears that exposure to affluent or talented classmates makes the most difference. The lower down the ability and class range the more this factor increases in importance. This was the most promising finding of the Coleman report, and inspired many of the moves towards 'bussing' in the United States. Thomas Pettigrew, one of the main advocates of bussing, pointed to the close association between class and ethnicity and drew the conclusion that the Coleman research supported his case. The evidence for bussing is, however, inconsistent and often confused, as for most educational strategies. Jencks (1972: 106) estimates that economic desegregation might raise poor whites' scores by 1 or 2 points on average, and that complete racial desegregation would reduce the gap in test scores between blacks and whites from 15 to 12 or 13 points. The Douglas (1964) study in Britain presents a strong case for connection between poor school conditions and deterioration of test scores, which could be linked to school 'climate' rather than to physical conditions. These are reported too by the Robbins Report (1963). It is doubtful though whether the differences are much greater than those reported in the American studies of Coleman and Jencks, since the selective system would tend to dramatize the differences between schools and to underplay those that would exist within schools in a comprehensive system. Nevertheless, the importance of obtaining a good social 'mix' or balance in schools and streams in classrooms appears to be the most promising area for experimentation and future research.

The causal fallacies of compensation

Many people may not be impressed by the sort of input–output approach of this section. What, after all, have measures of expenditure to do with careful and patient teaching? What have standardized test scores to do with personal growth? How can one really measure school quality without talking of the assumptions and ideologies of individual teachers? The answer is that all these objections may be valid, but that policy-makers have been forced to deal with the things that can be measured and justified to those who provide the means for change and improvement.

The logic behind the 'compensatory' model at the level of school resources is after all quite seductive. It is very easy to make the association between 'bad schools' and 'poor homes' and 'dumb kids', and to conclude that there must be a causal relationship in there somewhere. If we cannot change the homes then at least we can change the schools. If every child was housed in a purpose-built comprehensive school or in an attractive and modern primary school, perhaps the children would learn faster and the association between homes and stupidity would gradually disappear.

Despite the shortcomings of the statistical game of Jencks and others, at least it has shown the fallacies of this sort of reasoning. This fallacy of the 'compensatory' liberal model has been, on the analogy with the streamlined hospital, that an attractive plant staffed by qualified professionals would somehow cure the cognitive diseases of the slum. It is little wonder then that this kind of medical reasoning should have led to biologistic explanations of cognitive inequality – if something cannot be cured it might be hereditary. On the other hand, there are those who, like Halsey (1972), would like to knock down the conditions that produce underprivilege altogether, to abolish the social situations such as slums that lead to educational failure. As we saw in the first chapter, the tendency towards biological explanations on the one hand and class conflict and socially reproductive explanations on the other appear to be predictable responses to the failure of social science to explain outcomes in terms of educational treatments and public policies.

3 School quality and credentials

The influence of schooling on achievement needs to be distinguished from that on credentials and on life chances. Cognitive skills represent only one rung in the ladder of opportunity and it is quite clear that pupils of similar ability and achievement have different rates of success in obtaining credentials and jobs. There appear to be built-in balances, however, between the effects of types of schooling on credentials on the one hand and between family background on schooling on the other that diminish the egalitarian effects of educational expansion. This tendency for educational effects to cancel out is seen nowhere better perhaps than in a comparison between the selective system of Britain and the mainly common or comprehensive system of the United States. We shall look at this comparison in this section as it applies to the access of children of different abilities and backgrounds to credentials (i.e. educational opportunity). In the following section we will look at the access of children of different abilities and backgrounds to occupations (i.e. social opportunity).

One of the salient features of a US–British comparison is that while very small effects of school quality on achievement also holds for credentials in the US case, the opposite applies to Britain. Two quotations, one from Jencks (1972:159) and the other from Tuck (1974:149) who carried out a reanalysis of the Douglas data, may illustrate the difference:

> Qualitative differences between high schools seem to explain about 2 per cent of the variation in students' educational attainment. Unfortunately, we cannot say what qualities of school boost its college entrance rates and what qualities lower it. School resources do not appear to influence students' educational attainments at all. Attending school with bright, highly motivated classmates seems to have both positive and negative effects on a student's chances of attending college. (Jencks)

> It certainly seems as if the instinct of the advocates of the comprehensive system, that social class was not in itself a vital determinant of educational performance, has been shown to be correct. Even if the existing balance, and the strength of social indicators such as accent etc., remain the same, the alteration of educational institutions will bring about a significant change. (Tuck)

How might these two conclusions be reconciled? If, as Jencks claims (1972: 158), simply expanding the number of 'college track' places in American schools does not affect the class rates of college entrance, then can we expect that breaking down the institutional barriers to higher education represented by the different examination systems of selective schooling in England will be any more effective? As we have seen in the previous section, the rates of opportunity in getting onto a college track and in being 'selected' are much the same for children of the same background and ability. The question as to whether a similar pattern will be found in access to credentials remains to be examined in the light of the following evidence.

Provision and opportunity in Britain

There is a tradition of British research that is disposed to the expansion in the provision of 'true' secondary school education as a means of expanding the educational chances of working-class children. According to this tradition, associated with the research of Eggleston (1974) and later of Byrne, Williamson and Fletcher (1975), the class rates of educational attainment cannot be completely explained in terms of ability or of motivation. If there were more places at the secondary level that were designed to lead pupils into higher education, there would be more working-class children in these institutions. This tradition takes the local authority area as its unit of analysis, and is, therefore, different in approach to the studies of Jencks and of Coleman and of Plowden, which take the individual child as the unit of study.

The Byrne, Williamson and Fletcher study (*The Poverty of Education*, 1975) rejects Jencks' conclusions from this different perspective. The overwhelming conclusion of these researchers is that patterns of selective or extended course provision (i.e. of allowing movement to 'A' levels and to university) between local authorities have a very strong influence on rates of 'staying on'. This is so, they claim, even when social background variables are controlled for. They propose a 'socio-spatial' model of inequality to complement the individualistic analysis of Jencks and claim that sociologists should try to examine the political background of educational provision. An historical, administrative and structural account of educational provision, they say, will yield a different type of result.

This difference in emphasis and approach cannot be the whole explanation of the optimism of many British sociologists' hopes that a wider provision of comprehensive education will open wider avenues of ascent to the working-class child. The study of Tuck mentioned above also provides a case for the abolition of selection, even though it was based on an analysis of the careers of *individual* children. The study used statistical techniques similar to those of Jencks to estimate the effects of selective placement on credentials gained at school and at university for children of different sex, ability and background.

Tuck's study indicates several interesting effects of school placement on attainment, supporting her conclusion quoted above. She found that at each stage of the ladder (at 'O' and 'A' levels and at university) the type of school makes most difference to the pupil's success (though it should be noted that intelligence is 'absorbed' to a large extent by school type). Social class appears to be less important than both type of school and intelligence as a predictor of exam performance, and at university the role of intelligence is far less important than the type of school. In an analysis of the movement up the ladder of attainment (rather than of just the causal background to success at a particular level) it was found that the most important factor working against progress from 'O' to 'A' level was the type of secondary school. The next greatest handicap was 'being a girl', followed by social class and low ability. At the stage from 'A' level to university, sex became a far more important handicap and the influence of the other variable becomes relatively weaker.

Therefore, it is not simply the 'level of analysis' that influences the kinds of interpretations that sociologists draw from their data. The use of a 'socio-spatial' model appears to be not the only way to arrive at conclusions that, in the British case at least, oppose the negative findings of Jencks on the effects of the school environment on educational opportunity. How is this possible? Is the American system of 'tracking' very different from the British system of selection to different schools? Might one expect to find that a different way of organizing the progress of students through the secondary system that was not rigidly organized along institutional lines would allow greater opportunity – even if, as we saw, entry into these 'tracks' is determined by similar contributions of ability and social background?

This is the most important question confronting comprehensive reformers in Britain and in other countries that employ a 'sponsored' mode of organizing educational mobility. In order to answer it adequately we will have to look at English school systems under changes that have forced it in a more 'meritocratic' direction on the one hand, and on the other, at the probable changes that one could anticipate from its reorganization along the lines of the American system. As we shall see, there appear to be built-in checks in each case that diminish the egalitarian effect of reorganization or of reform.

Opportunity in Britain since world war II

Before looking at the second aspect of selective *vs.* comprehensive schooling, let us look at the historical changes in the selective system itself. What has been the change in the relationship between father's background and children's credentials in Britain over the century? The surprising answer to this question is that despite the greater emphasis on testing and the expansion of provision of both secondary and tertiary schooling since the second world war, the overall correlation between a child's attainment and his social background has remained about the same (Ridge, 1974; Kerckhoff, 1974). This applies, incidentally, to the US as well as to Britain (see Jencks, 1972: 138). Just as we saw in Chapter 2, that the amount of social opportunity has not appreciably changed, so too it appears that educational opportunity has been similarly stable. Why is this so?

There is no doubt that chances of higher educational attainment have improved for children of the working classes, but so they have for all classes. The working classes have been sending proportionally more children from their own groups to grammar school and to university, but it must be remembered that the base from which they began has been much smaller than that of the middle classes. Thus an improvement of say 10 per cent in the number of working-class children sent to university on a base of say 6 per thousand is not very great in absolute numbers, even if there are more working-class than middle-class children. If the middle classes send say 100 children per thousand to university, then an increase of 10 per cent is much more advantageous in relative terms and will tend to balance out any numerical superiority of the working classes. It is probably for these reasons that the class chances of university attendance in Britain, as noted by Little and Westergaard (1964), have changed little over this century. Despite the expansion of places, differential fertility between socio-economic groups and the introduction of more meritocratic forms of selection, the proportions of children from various backgrounds in higher education have not altered drastically. As Halsey (1972) says, 'the typical history of expansion in the 1950s and 1960s can be represented by a graph of inequality of attainment which has shifted markedly upwards without changing its slope'.

These findings appear to give little encouragement to those who emphasize the effects of school quality on educational opportunity. It is during the past quarter-century, it should be remembered, that the spread of resources and per-pupil expenditure have been equalized across classes. The programmes of mass secondary and further education have ensured that, as for the equalization of access to credentials as seen in the previous chapter, the proportion of money spent on the education of the poor has risen. With central government intervention in local education there is now far less inequality between regions as well. Selection has become ostensibly more meritocratic, and state intervention in all levels has added enormously to the general material quality of schooling, narrowing the resource gap between town and country, inner city and suburb, denominational and state schools. How then does one explain the stability of the correlation between attainment and family background, if one holds firmly to the interventionist model of provision?

Explaining stability of educational opportunity

The over-time changes in the British system suggest that there may be self-checking processes which balance out the egalitarian effects of expansion. These are rather different from the type of explanation noted above which says that the working class is always starting from behind. They have to do with the way the system reorganizes itself to fight off, as it were, the effects of egalitarian reform, to restore explicitly or by concealment, the bias towards the middle-class child. There are two types of mechanisms by which this appears to take place. The first is to do with the organization of routes to university through fee-paying and direct grant schools, as against state selective education. The second is to do with the ways in which informal pressures and procedures in the comprehensive school 'move in' to perform the same discriminatory function as the old forms of selection at 11+.

We could start with the anomaly noted by Halsey (1975b: 519), that despite the tendencies towards selection by ability in secondary school education since the second world war, the influence of the type of school has actually *increased* in predicting university entrance. It is now much easier for a middle-class boy who has been sent to an independent or direct grant school to get into university than it was before or just after the war. This confirms to some extent the rigidity in privileged routes noted in the previous chapter with regard to recruitment to élites in post-war Britain. The influence of the school has also increased in the state sector, with a narrowing of university entrance on the grammar schools as against the modern schools. Now since there is enormous class bias in the attendance at independent and direct grant schools, and a considerable degree of class bias in state selection, any strengthening of the link between the 'pecking order' of schools and university admission has worked in the interests of the middle class. This appears to explain some of the enduring bias in the British system.

Inequality and comprehensive schooling

However, what might be expected if, as many socialists in Britain wish to see, not only selective but independent education as well were to be abolished? Would a remodelling of the education system along the lines of the American or the Swedish models see a considerable decrease in the influence of class on credentials? We have seen already that the American system tends towards a kind of streaming at the age of sixteen and that the biases by ability and background are almost identical then as they are at eleven plus in Britain. There is a school of thought in Britain that is aware of the dangers of 'streaming under one roof' in an apparently comprehensive system. One researcher (Ford, 1969) has in fact shown that the biases towards social class may be even higher in the streaming practices of the comprehensive school than it was in the old selective and non-selective schools. Although there is some evidence that resources are more evenly spread in a comprehensive system, as mentioned earlier, there is no evidence that the rates of attainment are any better because of this. The hope that Ford expresses that 'superior educational opportunities' would even the race does not appear to have been fulfilled in practice.

There is a growing and increasingly difficult literature on the effects of comprehensive reorganization on examination success in English education (Eggleston, 1975). This literature is not very convincing or conclusive since it does not have a clear definition of what constitutes a comprehensive school because the rates of examination entrance are subject to historical and regional variation and because the effects of reorganization themselves have indeterminate effects on the way parents and pupils and teachers perceive and operate the system. One of the clearest ways of examining the effects of reorganization is to compare the patterns of opportunity between countries, one with a well-developed comprehensive system and one with an historic pattern of selection. It is for this reason that a comparison between the United States and Britain in its pre-comprehensive era (e.g. the 1950s) may be more valuable than an analysis of British districts undergoing reorganization.

Opportunity in Britain and in the US

The analysis of Kerckhoff (1974) provides the basis of such a comparison. Using different measures of educational attainment and drawing on various studies from both countries (notably that of Douglas for Britain), Kerckhoff comes to the conclusion not only that the patterns of selection to tracks or grammar schools are very similar, but so too are the class chances of attainment. It appears then the same kinds of students obtain credentials irrespective of whether they are 'sponsored' early or have to compete for them at every stage of their educational careers. This is not perhaps such an astounding finding, but it does raise some interesting problems as to how the two systems, so ideologically different, manage to produce the same pattern of opportunity.

The obvious answer to this problem is that the Americans have simply moved selection on a few years and that curriculum placement counts for the same in determining credentials as does selection in Britain. This is a deceptively simple answer, though it is one that naturally appeals to those who would like to abolish all forms of labelling, early or late, in the secondary school. It raises too many other problems to be accepted as it stands. In the first place, such a blatant form of final selection in a system where the vast majority of students are still at school violates the 'folk norm' of selection in the US. It would not be completely attenuated by the fact that it is possible in American schools to opt for 'credits' outside a particular stream in a manner impossible in the grammar school. In the second place, it appears that curriculum placement accounts for only a minor part of the relationship between test scores and a student's chances of entering college (Jencks, 1972: 145). In the British system selection plays a more prominent role, as Tuck's study indicates.

These objections to the simple explanation that curriculum placement has the same meaning as school selection would lead us to conclude that in an apparently freer, more egalitarian system there are less obvious forces at work which produce the same slope of class chances. In other words the 'contest' mode has probably many concealed mechanisms of discrimination which act cumulatively to produce similar patterns of ascent through education as those of the 'sponsored' mode. This may explain why American sociology seems, to British eyes, to be preoccupied with the effects of peer groups, teacher expectations and counselling practices. In Britain, it would appear that the biases of the system are much more explicit as may be easily seen from an inspection of institutional and government records. The notion of using counsellors to 'cool out' unsuitable children is quite foreign to such a system, as is the idea that bureaucratic practices of grading and selection can be subverted by peer group pressures.

Of the two quotations at the beginning of this section, it would appear then that Jencks' has more empirical appeal even for Britain. The expansion of grammar school places or their comprehensive school equivalent would probably not lead more working-class children to extend their educational careers. There may be some local instances where provision of such places would help to keep such children in school but, by and large, the forces governing educational choice do not appear to reside in the system itself – rather in the outside community. It would not appear likely either that the postponement of selection as in American schools alters the final slope of class chances. Again, the weakening of all forms of selection, that is by breaking down the distinctions between streams or routes within schools, may lead to a less explicit relationship between educational success and social origins but it would probably only serve to drive class influences underground.

What Jencks saw in individual schools in the United States would appear, therefore, to apply to the educational district or area in Britain. There is ultimately a need for the student to make a choice about 'staying on' which is not primarily governed by the way the secondary school system has organized the routes to college. It, therefore, appears that reformers would be better advised to consider all the influences of this choice and its place within the wider picture of social opportunity rather than to preoccupy themselves with the patterns of educational provision. (This point will be followed up in Chapter 5 when we consider the mechanisms of choice in social ascent through education.)

This comparison between British and American systems has only so far dealt with the educational aspect of the effects of the school environment. The models proposed by Turner deal with the whole life cycle, with the movement of individuals into and out of élites. Certainly if we are to deal adequately with the comprehensive issue, we shall have to examine the differences that comprehensive education may be expected to bring in promoting social as well as educational opportunity. Will comprehensive education make Britain less 'class-ridden' in this respect, will it raise the occupational aspirations of working-class children? Again it is here that the American model, based in popular belief on a good deal more social as well as educational opportunity, should be of great value for a comparative study. We turn, therefore, from an analysis of the effects of school quality which, as we have seen, are not very great on inequality in either cognitive skills or credentials to the wider question of its effects on social mobility.

4 School quality and life chances

An article comparing the process of status attainment in the United States and Britain (Treiman and Terrell, 1975) may help us to make some conclusions as to the differences in organizational patterns on life chances. The authors of this article look at the ways in which the two patterns of ascent typified by Turner may show up in the processes of mobility in the two societies. They suggest that the model of 'sponsored' mobility might imply a closer connection between educational attainment and consequent status attainment than does a system of 'contest' mobility. In investigating this and other hypotheses Treiman and Terrell go a long way to allaying some of the objections to the raw comparison between two different societies made by Kerckhoff on which the conclusions so far have been based.

Treiman and Terrell show that although British society is supposedly more organized around class values and extremes of class identity than is the American, there are, nevertheless, great similarities in the structural arrangements of both societies. They show, for example, that there is a very high correlation between the ranking of occupations, and also that the British occupational structure is not decidedly more working-class than the American. There are, however, great difficulties in comparing the educational structures of the two countries, since the British is much more complex, being a combination of school-leaving age, type of school attended and further and higher education. Nevertheless, they employ statistical techniques which combine these variables into a single educational measure, comparable with the American, which is usually expressed in terms of the highest grade of school completed.

The questions to which these authors address themselves are: (1) how closely is educational attainment related to occupational attainment in the United States and Britain? (2) to what extent does education serve as an agent of social mobility? (3) to what extent does education affect income, both directly and indirectly, through its effect on status?

The conclusions that these authors come to directly influence the ways in which comparisons of the organization of secondary education may affect social mobility as well as educational opportunity. They also have a bearing on the applicability of Jencks' model of inequality to Britain. The conclusions may be summarized as follows: (a) the association between social origins and educational attainment is about the same in the two countries; (b) despite the tendency of high-status sons to stay at school longer, education is largely independent of social origins and thus serves as an agent of social mobility; (c) the connection between a son's educational attainment and his occupational status is equally strong in the two countries; (d) despite 'radical differences' in the organization of educational ascent, the role of education in the transmission of status also appears to be very similar in the two countries; (e) there is considerably more non-educational transmission of status from father to son in Britain than in the US; (f) income is much more strongly determined by occupational status (and consequently by education) in Britain than in the US.

These findings, based on a study that is quite sensitive to the variations in each country's patterns of educational attainment and occupational structure, confirm the conclusions made so far about the expected effects of comprehensive organization on patterns of educational opportunity. However, they carry the comparison one stage further, and show that the same conclusions may also apply to social mobility. Despite the fact that there is more direct influence of a father's status on that of his son in Britain, it would appear that in each society the patterns of educational ascent are very similar. This would lead us, therefore, to be very sceptical of the belief that because Britain is more class conscious than the US and because it organizes its educational system around different norms of selection that its patterns of mobility should be any different. It should also make us sceptical of the claim that the reverse may be true; that a different system of educational mobility, more like the American, will make British society less 'class-ridden'.

'The old school tie'

Finally, it may be pointed out that here we have concentrated on the effect of school environment on life chances as it has affected the access to credentials. What about the 'old school tie' that supposedly makes a difference no matter whether the individual is educationally successful or not? The answer here appears to be negative once more, or at least that any direct difference that school quality does make is so small as to be very disputable. Again, for the US, Treiman and Terrell (1975 : 580–1) quote a number of findings which indicate that 'curriculum makes virtually no difference in expected occupation once college attendance is taken into account', and they conclude that 'it is overwhelmingly obvious that type of schooling has virtually no effect on occupational attainment in the United States independent of its influence on amount of schooling obtained'. Jencks (1972 : 190) too treats this direct influence as negligible and concludes that all of the influence of school quality on occupational status, direct and indirect, 'usually affects children's later status by only a couple of points'.

In Britain, where one would expect that access to information and job contacts would make a great deal more difference, again the direct effect of type of secondary school on occupational status appears to be very small. This was shown by Ridge (1974: table 3.6) in a reanalysis of some of the Glass data across three generations in the first half of the century. The main advantage of attending an independent or a selective school appears to be in the headstart it gives to acquiring the right kinds of credentials. As we saw in the previous sub-section, this can be considerable, and the channel of success seems to have become even narrower in the post-war period.

Conclusion

The overall impression of this chapter may indeed be that school environments make little difference to achievement, credentials and to life chances. Certainly there is very little that one can find among all this negative evidence which could be used as a purchase for some new, egalitarian reform. Differences in schooling appear merely to provide variations on patterns of attainment and mobility that seem to be fixed elsewhere. The school environment regulates these patterns but it does not change them.

The American evidence is only circumstantial for making conclusions about the probable effects of comprehensive schooling in Britain. It does not show that there is *not* going to be some basic change in educational mobility under the new system. What it does is to make the possibility that it will bring more equality appear rather remote. There is not a great deal more educational mobility in the US than in Britain, despite the radical differences in ideology and organization of secondary education in the two countries and despite the much higher rate of educational attainment in the US, amounting (on the average) to about three years more formal schooling. So in terms of occupational mobility what applies to the 'tightening bond' appears also to apply to school quality, and to the different patterns of educational provision.

These conclusions do not, of course, alter the fact that there may be other grounds for introducing comprehensive schooling, or seeking a more equitable pattern of expenditure. Nor do they provide ammunition for the 'right' who would like to see comprehensive schooling abandoned, any more than they do for the 'left' who would like to see it become the norm. What this analysis may have done is to show the futility of carrying ideological differences into areas where they have little practical effect.

There is perhaps a strong moral case for abolishing all forms of discriminatory consumption in areas of public service such as education and health care. However, these arguments in the case of education have in the past been a source of long political disputes that have often led their proponents to make assertions far outside the scope of the available evidence.

The recent evidence presented here would point to a search for new policies of opportunity that were not so closely linked to the more visible patterns of provision and expenditure. This analysis would suggest that there may be deep-seated tendencies in industrial societies that regulate the amount of social mobility and the class slope of educational attainment which have nothing to do with the overall level of expenditure or the way the school is organized. Indeed, it would appear that the more meritocratic system such as that seen in Britain since the war, and the more egalitarian system of the United States, both appear to produce the same rates of social and educational opportunity. Neither seem to provide a model for future reform.

We are, therefore, led to enquire what is the 'driving force' behind the patterns of educational and social attainment that appears to render them so intransigent. Is it perhaps the innate inequality of children from different classes that makes them do better at school no matter how good the teacher is or how the selective processes work? This is one explanation that cannot be ignored and it is one which is becoming increasingly debated in academic circles. We cannot afford to ignore this explanation even though as we shall see in the following chapter it may not be entirely convincing. We will, therefore, turn in Chapter 5 to an explanation of the structural arrangements which produce such great stability and such a large degree of individual randomness.

4

Genetics and inequality: the IQ debate

What causes inequality in educational outcomes – poor parents, bad schools or just plain inborn stupidity? We have just looked at the effects of the school environment and seen that this must be rejected as a main cause. If this is so, then one is obliged to ask how much of the variation is caused by the innate ability of the individual to exploit the educational system and thereby to achieve socially. Despite the fact that most of this variation occurs *within* families, there appears to be some variation *between* families as well. One is, therefore, led to ask how much of the variation in IQ is systematically transmitted by the class structure. If the environmental influences appeared to be weak in the transmission process (e.g. if identical twins reared apart ended up with the same IQ score), we might finally be able to account for the class and racial biases in outcomes with which we are all too familiar.

Such a biological explanation would have a good deal of attraction. It would neatly account for the failure of compensatory policies, as well as for the small effects of school quality. It would also explain why so many working-class children are able to 'get ahead' while at the same time inequality of outcomes between the classes is so persistent. It would also fit into the framework of the 'evolutionary liberal' model that has been at the basis of so much of educational thinking during this century. A revival of the thinking of the earlier welfare state would, therefore, provide an explanation for the failure of post-war reforms to abolish inequality.

There are, however, certain difficulties with such an explanation that make it rather questionable. Not only does it not adequately explain the slope of class and racial chances in education and economic success, it presents no real insights into educational practice. The inheritance of IQ debate, as we shall see, is almost completely irrelevant to the issue of inter-group differences. Not only is it empirically possible to demonstrate this, it is also possible to show that many of the geneticist arguments are logically misconstrued. It is a dangerous field for beginners and it is only a pity that what Jensen began as a cautious and academic argument should have been exaggerated into a bitter ideological debate about inequality at large and racial discrimination in particular. This debate has ranged far and wide over questions of educational expenditure and linguistic competence and even over academic freedom to do research into contentious issues.

It is very difficult because of the ideological component to discriminate between purely conservative (or 'traditional élitist') arguments based on the genetic differences of the classes, 'evolutionary liberal' arguments and those that derive from Herrnstein's model of the 'meritocracy'. As we saw in the first chapter, these all tend to be presented by conservatives of all persuasions when confronted by a single issue of policy such as comprehensive schooling, bussing or the reallocation of resources from rich families to poor families. Appeal to 'excellence' and 'traditional values' mingle with those of biological élitists in the *Black Papers* and in other such anthologies of conservative thought (e.g. Wilson, 1975). Even though these two strains are far apart, as may be seen in T. S. Eliot's (1948) condemnation of meritocracy, they present a common ideological front in the face of the left-wing challenge.

The debate has a central issue which may be summed up as follows. The 'right' say that educational opportunity and educational equality are two different things. Because children are innately unequal it is necessary to choose which one should inform policy. On the other hand, the 'left', mainly composed of those who hold to a class conflict model, claim that equality of opportunity is impossible without equality of condition. According to the protagonists of the 'left' the claim that ability is biologically inherited is simply a tawdry excuse for doing nothing. Who is correct? Are the reproductive forces of modern society embedded in biological inequality, or are there other mechanisms that carry out this process? We shall look more closely at the other explanations in the following chapter. As we shall see in the following discussion, the biological argument is seriously deficient. Let us first, however, deal with some common misapprehensions about the IQ issue, before looking at this argument in detail.

Some common misunderstandings in the IQ debate

Since the intelligence test is often not very different from the other tests of cognitive skills, and is often used in conjunction with them as in the 11+ examination, it may seem rather strange to think of an IQ score as inherited – like blue eyes or baldness. This analogy is the first source of confusion. The claims made by Jensen, Eysenck and Herrnstein that there is an 80 per cent inheritance factor have been interpreted by many people as if an *individual's* score could be split up into certain proportions. Thus, quite erroneously, it is sometimes thought that a person who receives an IQ score of 100 receives 80 of these points from his parents and the other 20 from his environment. This interpretation could not be further from the truth. It would be also quite erroneous to conclude that we can make estimates about the genetic factors in the scores of sub-populations (e.g. the children living in a London suburb) from what is observed for a population as a whole (e.g. all the children in England).

A heritability estimate is, therefore, a very tricky statistic. So tricky in fact that it cannot tell us anything really about individual children or even large groups of them. It may tell us that intelligence is in certain populations subject to the same pattern of inheritance as is height or weight or head length, but it tells us nothing about why Johnny is reading badly, or why boys in an inner-ring school tend to drop out early. We might be very sophisticated in making generalizations about populations but altogether ignorant about particular children, families, neighbourhoods, or even cities. As with physical growth, intellectual retardation might stem from malnutrition, even though we may claim that intelligence, like height, is highly heritable.

This confusion between the general and the particular points to a more serious weakness in the explanation of cognitive inequality by genetic arguments. This is that despite high estimates of heritability, we can never arrive at what *causes* difference in IQ scores. The estimates are simply *descriptions* of what goes on in a certain culture and in a certain set of social conditions. They provide no real explanation and are virtually useless in setting the limits of policy. Any heritability coefficient is, as Cronbach (1973) points out, 'a socio-cultural fact.' It is produced by a certain society and only has meaning within that society.

Since heritability differs from the other 'causes' of inequality, one cannot make inferences about policy in the way that it is possible for, say, the quality of the school environment. If, for example, we found that there was a larger inheritance factor for IQ than for scholastic achievement, we could not draw the conclusion that there was a greater scope for policy in boosting the one rather than the other. In the first place, small contributions of inheritance to scholastic achievement may be combining with environmental factors in ways that are very complex and inaccessible to intervention. In the second place, what *appears* as a genetic contribution, such as skin colour, may simply be caused by systematic discrimination against children with a certain trait such as blue eyes, red hair or black skin. The reasoning that goes along the line: 'If we equalized all environments there would be only 10 per cent less inequality in IQ' or 'if we equalized genes three-quarters of the inequality in incomes would persist' is, therefore, only statistical speculation. It tells us nothing of the social realities that bring it into existence.

The fact that the definition of ability and its causal explanation has nothing to do with genetics but with cultural and social arrangements is often forgotten, however. The issue is often confused with analogies to spatial blindness, mongolism and other specifically genetic defects where a 'cause' of retardation may be legitimately identified. The confusion between cultural and biological phenomena is not new to the testing movement which traces its origins from the eugenics debates of the turn of the century (Karier, 1972). Eysenck's attempt to give a neurological basis to IQ scores with examples of the EEG patterns of bright and dull subjects probably adds to this confusion. The temptation to look on IQ scores as immutable facts of nature is to be resisted, therefore, for all these reasons.

The prominence of the genetic explanation of failure since the publication of Jensen's (1969) long and authoritative article is quite understandable. Indeed, many of the misapprehensions in the debate have sprung from a misreading of Jensen. Certainly none of the confusions discussed so far can be blamed on anything that Jensen explicitly stated in this article. Rather they may be seen as ideological responses to a submerged and previously discredited type of thinking. At the end of the 1960s a wave of pessimism was sweeping educational circles as the 'compensatory' model which had guided so much of the reform at this time was seen to be unproductive. Planned intervention such as the Headstart programme was apparently impotent in the face of the overriding cognitive disadvantages of poor working-class children, since neither pre-school nor in-school programmes had any apparent long-term effect. It was small wonder then that Jensen's pollination of the theories of Burt across the Atlantic proved to be so effective.

Jensen's explanation of the failure of compensatory policies caught the conservative and disillusioned mood of the 1970s. Here was a simple and economical explanation of educational success. The limits of cognitive change in our culture were set allegedly by the patterns of inheritance. There was little point in the attempt to compensate for the environments of the poor since in all probability it was not the environment that was driving the 'engine' of inequality. Instead of continuing blindly with expensive experiments it would make much more sense to understand the mechanisms of inheritance, particularly as they affected the types of learning that seemed most appropriate for certain groups of children. The racial issue which was later to assume such prominence in this debate was, therefore, only marginal to Jensen's main theme.

It was in later debate and discussion that the famous 'fifteen point gap' between the average scores of black and white children in the US became the main point of discussion. There was not at any stage of the first article the explicit assertion that this 'gap' was also set by differences in the genetic potential of races. The publicity and pressure that followed the popular impression that this was indeed what Jensen was saying forced the issue. What was originally a cautious and academic proposal became explosive political material. Jensen consequently took a rather rigid position on this issue, and the debate was taken up by several polemicists – Eysenck, Shockley, Herrnstein, among others.

The explanation of the difference on average IQ scores goes as follows: if we assume that the inheritance factor is the same for blacks as it is for whites, then the widest mean environmental variation that would be observed between groups under normal limits of probability would be about 7 points. However, the observed difference is in fact between 12 and 15 points – apparently much too wide to be environmentally induced. This claim, of course, makes many assumptions about IQ tests, the applicability of inheritance estimates from one group to the other, and the types of statistical probability that should be acceptable in such conditions.

There has been a good deal of publicity and a great amount of controversy stirred up by the protagonists of this proposition and its opponents. As we shall see, however, most of the argumentation is peripheral to the explanation of the systematic and persistent class and racial biases in educational outcomes. Let us then examine the case made by the geneticists. It falls into two stages – educational and societal. At each stage, it may be seen, inequality has a biological basis. The argument runs as follows:

A Educational

(*a*) Test scores measure innate ability and
(*b*) accurately predict academic success.
(*c*) Most of the inequalities in educational outcomes can be explained by the heredity component in IQ scores and this sets limits on the effectiveness of intervention.
(*d*) Inequalities in educational outcomes of children from different backgrounds are transmitted by this heredity component.
(*e*) The educational system can be made more efficient if it recognizes inherited differences in ability between groups and classes and matches these to specific educational treatments.

B Societal

This argument is an expansion of 'A' into a wider model of 'the meritocracy':

(*f*) Since success is increasingly correlated with educational attainment and native ability, social inequalities increasingly reflect individual differences in the inheritance of IQ.

(*g*) There is, therefore, a real danger that society will sort itself into castes where educational differences will become the basis of stratification. Since the intellectually competent and privileged will marry among themselves, social and biological inheritance will become inseparable.

Genetics and educational disadvantage

(a) *Is ability innate?*

There is a good deal of evidence that cognitive inequality is broadly related to genetic background. Despite the fact that many liberals may wish to argue against this on all kinds of grounds, both moral and philosophical, within the terms that the geneticists argue, this conclusion seems inescapable. Jencks' (1972) 'Appendix A' is a deep technical discussion of the subject, at the end of which he concludes that for a white US population 'the best guess is that genotype explains about 45 per cent of the variance in IQ scores, that environment explains about 34 per cent and that the correlation between genotype and environment explains the remaining 20 per cent'. Transference of these estimates across populations is not permissible, nor, as noted above, is the direct application to any particular sub-population. The English studies of Burt show a higher inheritance factor, closer to 80 per cent. This, Jencks suggests, may be attributed to the greater heterogeneity of environments in the US. Accepting the fact that a large portion of the variance in intelligence is due to genetic factors does not, however, commit us to any of the other propositions set out above. It is very important, then, that the distinction between sociology and quantitative genetics be made very clear. It is when geneticists step out of their familiar role and speak on educational matters that confusion often arises, as indeed often happens too when educationists propose to become embroiled in the intricacies of 'twin' studies.

(b) *Do IQ scores accurately predict academic success?*

If there is this fairly stable, heritable property called intelligence, what use can it be put to? Since the tests were validated against performance in schools and in large organizations one might expect that an individual's IQ score would be a very accurate predictor of his success. Indeed, it might appear so, but this must be modified by the extreme inaccuracy that characterizes social science predictions in general. Whereas most associations in this area normally yield correlation coefficients of between ·4 to ·5 at best, it is not unusual to find correlations between ·6 and ·7 in predictions from IQ scores. It would be misguided, however, to conclude that this was anything approaching perfect prediction. In most cases only about a *half* of the variation is captured by such relatively high correlations. The IQ test scores are better than most 'natural' predictors of attainment such as school grades, because they have been designed to fulfil this purpose. In real life, however, there are just too many unknowns in the attainment process – personality characteristics, environmental and instructional factors, 'luck' in exams – for one to rely on test scores as a single valid indicator of educational outcomes.

On the other side of the coin it is possible to argue that we should design our educational environments so that outcomes are more highly correlated with IQ scores than they are at present. This was, of course, the aim of sociologists during the 1950s and 1960s – to reduce the 'wastage' of talent. However, despite the efforts of social scientists to measure, locate and redirect talent, such wastage persists. This would lead one to suppose that there are other causes of early leaving or 'dropping out' than low ability, and that these are not so amenable to social engineering.

The extent of this wastage is delineated by Jencks (1972 : 145) for the US and by Floud (1961) for Britain. In the US, for example, Jencks estimates that a 15 point test score difference is associated with only a 4 per cent increase in chances of entering college. The findings of Floud, based on the National Service Survey (Crowther Report, 1960), indicated the wastage in the top ability groups: 'Of the entire group of recruits, only 2 per cent were graduates or had achieved a comparable educational qualification. This élite accounted for less than one in five (18 per cent) of the young men in the top ability group, and for a minute proportion (1 per cent) of those in the second.'

There are technical reasons for this poor prediction from above average ability to academic success. One of these is the 'twisted pear' effect (Fisher, 1959) which denotes the fact that prediction in outcomes becomes increasingly difficult as we move up the scale of ability or of any other predictor variable. Higher ability, in other words, is not as good a predictor of college or university attendance as lower ability is of 'dropping out'. It would seem rather futile then to expect a 'meritocracy' by conventional methods of expanding opportunity since there seem to be inbuilt features of social prediction that militate against such an outcome. Therefore, while it may be justifiable to use test scores for the extraction of lower ability groups, their applicability to the average and above average student would seem to be rather questionable. A perfect match between scores and attainment would indicate a 'meritocracy' (in the original sense of Michael Young (1958), rather than of Richard Herrnstein), where the test score has become the tyrant of all social relationships. This is surely not a very desirable prospect, and it is not one which is envisaged by most of the proponents of the innateness of intelligence.

We may, therefore, conclude that although intelligence test scores provide the best available basis for predicting educational success, they are far from perfect. Even if one resolved the question of their unreliability, which led to their discrediting in the 1950s, it is doubtful whether they could ever explain more than about a half of the inequality in credentials. Without massive social engineering that would threaten conventional liberties of educational choice, it is unlikely that this degree of accuracy could be improved.

(c) *How much of the inequality in educational outcomes is due to the inheritance of intelligence?*

This question is almost entirely academic because as we have seen, the estimate of a 'contribution' to IQ will tell us nothing about causal mechanisms in the acquisition of intelligence. Therefore, a larger or a smaller inheritance component in scholastic performance (achievement) or in credentials will be similarly useless in making conclusions about the probable effectiveness of compensatory schemes to boost these. In the comparative sense, then, we cannot conclude that a lower heritability estimate for these outcomes will indicate that intervention is likely to be more effective than it has been in the area of measured ability. Nevertheless, if one makes the questionable assumption that some causal implications do reside in these estimates, it will appear that the genetic argument is diminished in its own terms.

The fact that ability tends to be inherited leads to the plausible conclusion that a good deal of the differences in educational outcomes is due to genetic advantage. Such a conclusion would, however, be mistaken, even if a causal relationship were involved with the contribution of inheritance. In the first place as we have seen, test scores are not perfect predictors of academic success. If the 40–60 per cent of the variance that they did explain in credentials were the result of genetic 'causes', then it is clear that even with the most generous estimate of heritability (80 per cent) over half of the inequalities in credentials would still be unaccounted for. With respect to achievement, which is, of course, much more closely linked to IQ than credentials, Jensen (1967: 153) himself concludes that 'in general individual differences in scholastic performance are determined less than half as much by heredity than are individual differences in intelligence'.

On examination then, we find that the contribution of the IQ genotype to educational outcomes is not large enough to be regarded as a satisfactory theory of inequality. In fact, when we examine the inheritance component in these outcomes, rather than in measured intelligence, we find that, even in Jensen's own terms, the ratio is reversed in favour of the environmental contribution. By one of Jensen's estimates (1967: 153), the 80/20 ratio is completely reversed in the case of scholastic performance. One must, therefore, have severe doubts about the relevance of the inherited component in IQ scores to other educational outcomes.

(d) *How valid are genetic explanations of class and racial differences in measured ability?*

Let us leave the prediction from test scores for a moment and try to explain the social and ethnic differences in the so-called 'phenotype' (IQ) itself. These differences between group averages in measured ability have provided several writers with a theory of educational failure and of the consequent biases in class and ethnic rates of attainment. Certain groups of children, it is held by these writers, come from socio-economic or ethnic groups that are genetically inferior in the aspect of intelligence. The following extract from an article by Richard Lynn (who could probably be labelled as a 'traditional élitist' in the above terminology), may serve as an example:

> The effect of this flexible social system is that the more intelligent genetic strains must have tended to become

concentrated in the middle class. Of course this is only a tendency and does not apply to every single middle-class child. Some unintelligent children continue to be born into the middle class and some highly intelligent children into the working class. Nevertheless, on the average innate class differences in intelligence must certainly exist. They can be demonstrated directly by examining the IQs of adopted children. Those born to middle-class parents tend to be more intelligent than those born to working-class parents.

Now as we have already seen, no-one would claim that skin colour or low social origins equal poor genetic potential at the individual level, the refutation of the case of Lynn (or, in the racial case, of Jensen and of Eysenck) must be based on population terms. We have also seen that it is not justifiable to apply heritability estimates to sub-populations nor to transfer these estimates to other populations. Yet this is indeed what the geneticist case rests on. In the following discussion, however, it may be shown that even when these very high estimates are assumed to apply to black or to working-class children, it is still possible to show the difficulty of the geneticist position. We will examine the IQ 'gap' (i) between social classes and (ii) between white and black populations.

(i) *The socio-economic gap*. It is not difficult to show how untenable are the arguments, such as those of Lynn, that children inherit their intelligence scores through the biological differences between socio-economic groups. Intelligence scores are first of all susceptible to the well-known statistical phenomenon of the 'regression to the mean', an expression that denotes the tendency of extremes to revert back to the population average. This phenomenon is very clearly explained by Eysenck (1973) himself in a refutation of Herrnstein's theory of meritocracy. Because of this, the IQ scores of children of genetically advantaged parents will always tend to resemble the average more than do those of their parents.

The rather low correlation between children's social background and their IQ scores is demonstrated perhaps best of all by Burt (1961) for an English population. Despite the gap between extremes of social background there is in fact about nine times more cognitive inequality within groups of children of the same socio-economic background than there is between them. How much of this association could be construed as genetic and how much could be environmental in origin? Even if we take a very high estimate of heritability and a very low estimate of environmental influences caused by differences in social background, we would find that most of the association between background and IQ would *still* be environmental. In other words, the association between a child's IQ genotype and his parents' socio-economic status is very small indeed, so small, in fact, that any possibility of a cycle of deprivation forming because of biological inheritance of cognitive ability must be discounted (see Appendix to this chapter).

(ii) *The ethnic gap*. The second argument for inter-ethnic differences, particularly between black and white populations in the US, may be shown to be equally untenable. The scale of the 'gap' is quite large – about fifteen points or one standard deviation, much larger than for that between broad groupings of middle-class and working-class children. Here at least, the geneticists argue, is a disparity that is well beyond the limits of normal statistical probability. While often conceding the weak association between social background and IQ genotype, these writers would claim that for race the relationship is too strong to be ignored.

This argument has a good deal of appeal in some circles, but it rests on questionable premises: (*a*) that the size of the inheritance factor is indeed 80 per cent for white US populations; (*b*) that the inheritance factor for a sub-population (blacks of the US) is the same as for white populations; (*c*) that highly heritable characteristics will not show wide variations in average un-standardized levels at different stages of historical development. These may sound like very technical objections, but really they can be expressed very simply. Let us take them one by one:

(*a*) There is great dispute about what is the degree of inheritance of IQ in the US. Different methods of estimation yield widely discrepant ratios. Jencks' (1972:315) conclusion, after examining the studies of children with different degrees of relatedness reared under different conditions, is very tentative. The 'best guess', of a 45 per cent contribution from genotype is qualified by the statement about the chances of error: 'In gamblers' terms, this means we think the chances are about two out of three that the heritability of IQ scores, as we have defined the term, is between 0·35 and 0·55, and that we think that the chances are about 19 out of 20 that heritability is between 0·25 and 0·65.' If the heritability for blacks were the same as for whites, it would not be difficult to account for the IQ 'gap' by environmental differences using these estimates. The 80 per cent (0·8) factor found in English populations does not, therefore, seem to apply to the US. (*b*) The second point may show the difficulty of making even these much lower estimates 'stick' for different groups or sub-populations. The geneticist case rests here on the premise that blacks and whites would not differ in any important biological characteristic, therefore what 'causes' intelligence in the one case also 'causes' it in the other. This reasoning is fallacious because, as we have seen, the amount of heritability observed in one population has nothing necessarily to do with the amount in the other. There is no 'causal' relationship in the variations observed, simply associations. These may be entirely fortuitous and can yield different degrees of heritability, even in populations that are biologically similar.

As yet we have no estimate of the inheritance factor of IQ for black populations. If we did, there would still be difficulties in making any conclusions about the superiority of the IQ genotype for one group as against the other, since the environmental influences are impossible to 'control for' in any scientific way. It is almost impossible, for example, to 'partial out' the effects of prejudice for which the IQ 'gap' is not so great. If a study were perceptions and habits of the population. It is very difficult to imagine an experiment in which prior conceptions of cultural inferiority (possibly nurtured to some extent by the present debate) did not have an influence on the outcome.

It may be argued by the geneticists at this point that a degree of special pleading for the environmentalist position is being used. There are, after all, many other ethnic groups that experience prejudice for which the IQ gap is not so great. If a study were carried out which showed that for blacks in the US (or for black West Indians in Britain) there was indeed a high inheritance factor, would it not follow that the variation caused by the environment would be too small to account for this gap? After all, if the compensatory reformers have been willing to learn from the failure of their experiments in the classrooms, should they not also allow for the very slight effect that any change in environments may be expected to exert *outside* the school? Would it not then be demonstrated once and for all that inter-racial differences in learning do stem from genetic causes?

(*c*) So far we have queried the applicability of the 80 per cent figure to black populations, but accepting this figure does not prove that the observed IQ 'gap' is necessarily caused by genetic differences. High heritability of a characteristic does not mean that any observed difference is always caused by underlying differences in genotype. Historical changes can push the observed differences between generations far beyond the limits of probability set at any one time. This is well illustrated with respect to height which is almost perfectly heritable. Tizard (1975) demonstrated how the average height of London school boys, drawn from a relatively stable genetic 'pool' rose during this century (1909–52) by about 10 centimetres. However, the 'environmental effect' is only about 1·5 centimetres. This is only about a seventh of the observed difference (i.e. 10·2/1·47) while the IQ gap between blacks and whites is, as we saw, about double that of the 'environmental effect' (15/6·72).

Does this mean that we should conclude that there have been genetic changes in London, and that the genotype of boys measured in 1952 is substantially different from that of boys in 1909? Tizard, applying this question to the IQ 'gap', concludes that: 'It seems not unreasonable to argue that after two centuries of oppression, American blacks may be a generation or more behind in the intellectual diet that nurtures intelligence.' Since, as Jencks (1972:82) points out, the scores of white Army recruits rose by 9 to 12 points between 1918 and 1943, it would seem that any imputation of genetic inferiority on the basis of the observed difference in the average IQ scores of the different ethnic groups must be considered at best rather speculative.

(e) *Can estimate of the IQ genotype inform educational practice?*

If the IQ test is an imperfect predictor of educational outcomes, if the genetic basis of these outcomes is small, and if group differences in IQ genotype are infinitesimal or unknown, are there any grounds for using estimates of the IQ genotype as a basis for teaching or policy-making? It may seem curious in the light of the development of the debate that Jensen (1975:62) states that he knows of 'no principles of psychology or education that would warrant the consideration of either racial or social identity *per se* as at all relevant to educational treatment'. Jensen's aim is apparently to deal with variations in ability on the same basis as schools now deal with those among siblings reared together. The variation here is almost the same as that of the population at large – about 13 points. Jensen, therefore, sees no reason to change conventional approaches to inter-group differences. He would wish to see rather that biological bases of cognitive ability were recognized at an individual level and appropriate treatments were devised. In other words, Jensen does not indicate here (or in his longer treatment of the subject, *Education and Group Differences*, 1973) how a knowledge of racial or other inter-group genetic factors can be of much practical help in setting educational goals. Most of his discussion is not about the diversity between classes and ethnic groups, but of that within them. Jensen appears, therefore, to be in practice an 'evolutionary liberal' whose ideas have become mingled with the ideological rhetoric of other models.

This is perhaps unfortunate, but the wider social and political implications of the rhetoric which Jensen himself wields are not to be ignored. Indeed, a case could be made that, in the light of the evidence which the geneticists have produced, the ideological overtones are self-indulgent, and even irresponsible. The effect of Jensen's (and of Eysenck's) attempts to individualize failure and to give it a biological basis have been constructed by many observers as a justification for the inequality in group outcomes. In other words, the emphasis on the permanence of the IQ score allows group differences to re-appear by the back door, even though they have very little or no scientific basis in genetic theory. It is ironic in this respect that the pre-industrial fantasies of the extreme 'right' as well as the spectral visions of the 'meritocrats' can both find sustenance at the same ambiguous source.

It should be pointed out that most of the arguments and evidence in this section have been drawn from the writings of geneticists themselves. It has appeared that far from being, as they claim, the bearers of 'bad news' about inequality the genetic theorists have very little to say at all about inequality. None of their explanations of educability have much to do with practice, except to reinforce the well-accepted impression that conventional liberal approaches to reform have failed. As far as providing a basis for re-interpreting this failure as a result of its systematic biological relationship with the patterns of class and ethnicity, they fall down on their own terms. The explanation of the revival of the biological case, therefore, is probably to be found within the socio-political climate of the 1970s, rather than in the revelation of any new or pertinent evidence of why working-class or minority group children fail.

Genetics and 'the meritocracy'

Associated with the nature/nurture issue of cognitive advantage is the extension of the debate to include all forms of social stratification as the effects of IQ genotype work their way into the social structure of the future. This argument has been epitomized by Herrnstein's syllogism of the 'meritocracy' quoted in the first chapter, p. 30. The argument of Herrnstein neatly confronts left-wing and liberal reformers with the logical outcomes of their action. As school environments become more equal owing to compensatory provision, as the ascriptive criteria of sex, ethnicity and social background are winnowed away for occupational entrance then the only remaining differences that matter will be genetic in origin. This is a clever and, to some people, frightening argument. It rests on the assumption, of course, that there are changes towards selection by merit, that environmental differences are being compensated for and that IQ is inherited through the class structure.

We have already seen that the 'regression to the mean' effects undermine any tendency for a biologically inherited class structure to form. There is no inevitability in this direction, nor will putting the 'right' people on 'the pill', as some conservatives have claimed, make much difference to the incidence of intellectual incompetence. We have seen too that the effects of background on educational outcomes have not altered very much, nor have the general patterns of status inheritance. It is unlikely then that modern stratification systems are changing in the manner predicted by Herrnstein's 'embattled' syllogism.

This syllogism is, moreover, not valid, as has been pointed out by Block and Dworkin (1974): because a hereditary characteristic is necessary for eligibility for success it does not follow that every eligible person is successful. It may be that the *sufficient* (as distinct from the *necessary*) condition is environmental. Therefore, Herrnstein's second premise that success requires certain mental capacities does not lead necessarily to the conclusion that success is heritable. It could be that the condition for eligibility is a normal IQ genotype but that, in order to be successful, people with this genetic equipment need to have grown up in a very stimulating environment. Admittedly this is all very abstruse but it illustrates once more, if it were needed, the fallacious conclusions that may be drawn by ignoring the causal mechanisms of social selection.

We may still, however, examine the empirical validity of the syllogism, particularly in those aspects which have not been touched on in detail so far. Let us follow out then each of the two remaining points made at the beginning of this chapter.

(f) *Is the relationship between IQ and occupational status becoming any tighter?*

The moderate correlation between measured ability and status can be looked at in two ways, as an external proof of the fairness of the present occupational structure or as an artefact of the test itself. From the second perspective this correlation indicates not the inevitability of meritocracy but the assumptions of the testers themselves. Even then one might expect that selection could be a little more efficient than it appears to be.

Let us look first at some of the evidence about the occupational distribution of ability in modern Britain from the work of Burt. Burt (1961) used a rather unusual definition of occupational status which was based on neither prestige nor income but on the 'ability required for work'. Although in fact this is rather like a scale of educational attainment, the amount of unpredictability is still fairly large. Burt (1961 : table v) found that 'only 55 per cent of the population could be regarded as correctly placed if intelligence were the sole criterion'. This distortion, a kind of inversion of the 'twisted pear' mentioned above, appears to be greatest in the lower and middle ranks of the occupational scale. One finds in Burt's tabulation of occupation and intelligence, for example, that no member of the lowest ability group is below the ability threshold for his class, but over a quarter are above. On the other hand, for the upper occupational gradings, almost a half are below the threshold but only 8·3 per cent are above.

By analogy to the 'tightening bond' of education and jobs, we must look at this relationship over time. We find too, that as for the 'tightening bond' the reward structure does not appear to be becoming more closely related to cognitive ability. As for credentials, a higher level of absolute performance does not entail a tighter relationship with rewards. The dependence of status on intelligence as measured among US army recruits in the two world wars was much the same, even though the average recruit of the second war would have scored above 82 per cent of his comrades in the first (Jencks, 1972:204). For ability, as for credentials, it appears that a higher absolute level of competence or achievement does not mean that the class structure is becoming more meritocratic. The 'escalator' effect mentioned in Chapter 2 would appear to apply to IQ as well!

For these reasons, therefore, the claim that IQ genotype is becoming more closely linked with occupational status (or with income) appears to have very little empirical ground, whatever the logical status of Herrnstein's syllogism. There is no evidence of any change towards a tighter relationship between ability and life chances mediated as, the model proposes, through a more meritocratic, achievement-oriented selection process. The biblical statement that 'time and chance happeneth to all men' – regardless of their talents – would seem to be as apt now as at any period of history. If British experience is typical, the last few years have indeed shown perhaps a weakening of the meritocratic ties as the income structure has been reshaped by inflation and pay policies. This would suggest that for the moment at least, the 'meritocratic' model has been put into reverse.

(g) *Is there a danger of educational castes forming in economically advanced societies?*

Given that most of the evidence of genetically based inequalities is so inconclusive or inadequate, how seriously can we take the claim that we may be entering an era where there is a 'virtual caste-system with families sustaining their position on the social ladder from generation to generation as parents and children are more alike in their essential features' (Herrnstein, 1971)? One of the best refutations of this argument is that of Eysenck, in his book *The Inequality of Man* (1973) and in a shorter form in the *New Society* article (also 1973). Just as we saw in the section on the 'socio-economic gap', the possibility of a caste system arising biologically is extremely remote since its genetic transmission is tempered by regression effects.

This may now be supplemented by the evidence from the preceding section to demonstrate that a tightening chain from parental IQ through a child's genotype, to educational and occupational attainment is very difficult to imagine indeed. Not only are the relationships here apparently stable, but the chain of inheritance involves such a long association of probabilities that any kind of biological closure of the classes is resisted by the process itself. Since even a 'meritocracy' must continually re-sort itself, the 'spectre' that Herrnstein advances is something of a myth.

Conclusion

In view of this discussion, how might one explain what an editorial in *Social Policy* (1972–3) describes as 'the lingering infatuation with IQ'? In the same issue some attempt to answer this question is made by Bowles and Gintis in a radical critique of the place of IQ in the political economy of capitalist America. The theme of their article is that 'IQ-ism' and not simply the IQ score itself should be the theme of the present debate. The former implies the ideological overtones that are, according to these authors, falsely imputed to the scores by the popular imagination. The function of testing is to make social control and the reproduction of the class system appear to be 'value free' and meritocratic. Most people have accepted that IQ scores are closely linked to achievement, but, in fact, these authors claim the causal relationship is very weak when other background characteristics are controlled for.

The argument of Bowles and Gintis is parallel to the 'sociological' explanation of credentials described earlier, and can be seen as a 'class conflict' attack on the premises of the liberal welfare state (see also *Schooling in Capitalist America*, 1976, by these authors). In this model the failure of compensatory policies to boost the IQ scores of the disadvantaged is only a red herring from the important issues of inequality – wealth, power and the restriction of true opportunity. The interconnectedness of all of the dimensions of inequality outlined in the first chapter is reinforced by the Bowles and Gintis analysis, though one may disagree with its conclusions. The root cause of inequality they point to is hidden among all of the others and has to do with the power relationships between groups rather than with the distribution of individuals across social categories. It is very difficult to find 'objective' evidence of this hidden factor, as it is to suppose any conventional remedy for the inequality they perceive in capitalist society.

In this 'class conflict' model we are, therefore, left with subjective and rather ideologically tinged explanations of inequality. Cognitive inequality has become 'IQ-ism', educational attainment has become 'credentialism' and opportunity has become a covert form of 'social reproduction'. Admitted that there are biases in the educational system, and that these biases as we have seen seem to be ingrained in the whole process of attainment, we are *still* left with the problem of explaining the exact mechanisms that maintain the mobility process in such equilibrium. If ever there is to be some reform, it cannot come by invective or rhetoric, whether it originates from the 'right' or from the 'left'. We must, therefore, turn in the following chapter to the problem of explicating these mechanisms of social mobility more precisely.

Appendix to Chapter 4: A note on the genetic basis of the cycle of deprivation in Great Britain

For those who may be yet unconvinced as to the very marginal role of genetic factors in educational and consequently in social attainment, the following discussion may be of interest. This discussion is based on a path diagram (Fig. 4:1) which synthesizes the findings of a number of studies (Table 4:1) of social background and success in post-war Britain. From this model it is possible to investigate the contribution of genetic factors in the acquisition of ability to the socially and educationally transmitted cycle of deprivation.

Before we go on to look at the results of the analysis perhaps a few technical notes are in order. In three instances it has been necessary to use correlations based on American samples where British data is either unavailable or unsuitable. In neither of these instances, however, is there any reason to believe that these estimates are so much in error as to alter substantially the conclusions drawn from the model here. Moreover, in the light of the very high degree of similarity in the role of ability and family size in educational and occupational attainment in Britain and in the US (see discussion in Chapter 3) it would seem that the importation of these three coefficients is permissible, at least for the time being.

Where there has been any room for discretion in choosing between different estimates of the same relationship, I have preferred one that showed a 'meritocratic' bias. This applied in two instances: in the choice of an estimate of the heritability of IQ where the Burt/Jensen figure of 81 per cent (·9) was used, and in the use of a slightly higher estimate of the correlation between educational attainment (age on leaving school) and son's occupational status than that given by Treiman and Terrell (1975: Table 3). There has been no attempt to revise or adjust upwards the correlation coefficients. The effect of this, as with the above decision, has been to exaggerate the influence of IQ genotype in the model. Any inferences, therefore, probably yield the highest values that one can obtain for the 'meritocratic' case. ('Social background' as used below refers to a factor composed of father's occupational status, father's educational level, and family size.)

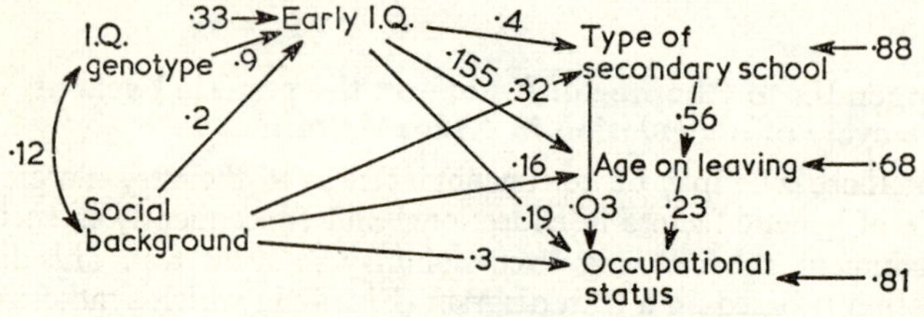

Fig. 4.1 A path diagram of status attainment for males in post-war Britain

Given the strong 'meritocratic' assumptions built into the model, what can it tell us about the pattern of inherited deprivation (or similarly that of inherited privilege) among post-war males in Britain?

For those who claim a strong genetic link in this pattern, the results are indeed discouraging. If we break down the association between the son's background and his achieved status, then it appears that only a tiny proportion (7 per cent at most) is attributable to the fact that boys from a higher social background also tend to have a higher genetic potential for doing well at school. This is only about a half of the contribution to the cycle made by a boy's environmentally inherited IQ, even allowing for the 81 per cent inheritance factor. Both of these might be compared with the relatively enormous influence which does not come via schooling or ability, but is rather transmitted directly from family to son (over 60 per cent). This influence might depend on 'string-pulling', the inheritance of wealth or property, or on a host of other factors that facilitate the cycle of transmitted advantage.

The same pattern emerges too when we break down the cycle of educational advantage. This is relevant, because, even in a 'true' meritocracy where a credential might give an assured status, the contribution of genetic factors is again quite slight. Only about 9 per cent of the class chances in attainment, as

Table 4.1 *Correlation matrix of variables included in Fig. 4.1*

	1	2	3	4	5	6
1 Social background	1·00	·12[g]	·31[a]	·443[a]	·45[a]	·48[b/c]
2 IQ genotype		1·00	—	—	—	—
3 Early IQ			1·00	·478[a]	·467[a]	·41[c]
4 Type of secondary school				1·00	·704[f]	·42[e]
5 Age on leaving					1·00	·48[d]
6 Occupational status						1·00

[a] Kerckhoff (1974: 195–6) based on Douglas (1964: 1968)
[b] Ridge (1974: Table 3.5)
[c] Duncan, Featherman and Duncan (1972: Fig. 5.9)
[d] Based on Macdonald (1974: Table 6.1). In Ridge (ed.)
[e] Halsey (1975a: 32)
[f] Based on Table 11 National Service Survey (Crowther, Vol. II: 131)
[g] Bowles (1972: 13) based on Jensen estimate of *h*

measured here, can be put down to differences in genetic inheritance of IQ. This compares very unfavourably with the 40 per cent of the cycle attributable to the influence of 'type of secondary school' (i.e. fee-paying or selective as against non selective or non fee-paying). This refers to the tendency of boys from a high social background to stay on at school, even though they are no brighter than their social equals, simply because they have been able to enter a 'better' secondary school. Conversely, it refers to the extent that boys of a lower social background will tend to 'drop out' earlier, even after controlling for their ability, because they were not 'selected' or because they were unable to get into a fee-paying school. Again, in connection with this educational pattern, it is interesting to note that fully a third (34 per cent) of the association between background and attainment is attributable neither to the higher ability of boys from higher social backgrounds, nor to the tendency of such boys to get into more favourable schools. Like the direct effect of background on son's status, this direct causal link between social background and attainment needs to be explicated and may have a good deal of relevance to the model of educational choice discussed in Chapters 5 and 6.

For all these reasons, therefore, it would appear that, compared with the massive constraints of family environment and of educational and social opportunity, the contribution of genetic factors in a cycle of transmitted deprivation or privilege palls to insignificance. Never once, even under these highly favourable assumptions, does it contribute more than 10 per cent to the process of transmission. It would appear that those who argue for a genetic basis to cycles of deprivation have only very slight empirical evidence for their case, and may be indeed distracting attention from areas where a less pessimistic social theory could inform policy.

5

Social background and attainment

So far we have said very little about the influence of 'the home' or 'the family' on patterns of educational and occupational attainment. Of course, there has been frequent mention of 'social background' but this has not been very closely specified. It would appear that this is about the only dimension left that may be able to help us to pin down the precise causes of educational inequality. In the two preceding chapters we have seen that the school environment is not a powerful influence and that inherited ability, although perhaps a small determinant of individual success at school, is distributed far too randomly to tell us anything about the way in which social inequality is created and perpetuated through the school system.

Probably more is known in this than in any other area of the sociology of educational inequality. A 'good' home, irrespective of its position in the social order, has been found by many research studies, to be the most powerful determinant of scholastic achievement and of educational attainment. A wide variety of studies have attested to the influence of cultural stimulation, housing conditions and family size, child-rearing practices and the values and attitudes of the parents on success at school (see Banks, 1976, especially Chapters 4 and 5).

Despite the enormous detail and care of these studies, many

sociologists have felt dissatisfied with their results. They appear to have broken up the clear divisions of social class and occupational position into tiny fragments and to have obscured the influence of the wider social structure. Again, they do not lead to very clear directions for educational policy. What, after all, can be done about the culture of the home if the father is out of work, if there is little encouragement from the peer group and if a sense of failure dominates the social life of the community. There is a real danger then that an emphasis on 'the home' will lead us to forget the socio-political environment. For this reason the emphasis will be on 'social' rather than 'family' background, although the two frequently overlap.

There is another problem too attached to the influence of social origins. That is, how the influence of the family works its way through the school into the child's occupational chances. We have seen that the occupational structure is fairly 'open', that is, more social mobility than immobility appears to be a characteristic of industrial societies. We have also seen that there is a good deal of apparent randomness in the way people with the same background and the same credentials arrive at different points of the social hierarchy. So just stopping at the influence of social background on school success will not be sufficient for explaining occupational and economic attainment. We need to show how social background, indirectly or directly, makes it easier for children to inherit the position of their father. The stability of the influence of social background on both educational success noted in the second and third chapters might make us look for systematic tendencies behind the 'luck of the rich'.

We need, therefore, to look very closely at the problems of translating the biases of the social structure into educational records and life chances of individual pupils. It is all too easy to dismiss the studies based on individual characteristics such as those of Coleman, Plowden or Jencks as 'bourgeois'. On the other hand, there is a danger of trivializing the influence of class by using a myriad of small scales of individual aspirations and family attitudes. We must try to explain the connection between structure and biography, otherwise many of the myths of educational inequality discussed above may persist. The task will not be easy, but it is a necessary endeavour if we are to find a new basis for formulating viable policies of liberal reform.

It may be helpful to think of the approaches outlined in the code' was a part of the 'culture of poverty' and that this prevented the working-class child from participating in the culture of the school. One could also claim that such a mechanism could help to explain what constituted a 'good home' regardless of Bernstein's proposal to link it to the divisions of the class structure. Finally, one could claim that Bernstein had hit upon a very important aspect of 'cultural capital' and that his theory of codes far from being a conservative 'culture of poverty' approach might reveal how the advantages of the rich are conveyed by cultural, as distinct from merely physical, processes. It is not difficult to see why Bernstein is called an arch-conservative by some of his critics, though he claims some intellectual allegiance to Marx. The reader is referred to Davies' volume in this series (*Social Control and Education*, 1976, ch. 7) for further discussion on this point.

Apart from the theoretical and ideological confusion that surrounds this area, it is very difficult to see much value in any one of the theses put forward. Like the geneticist position, they gain most of their impetus from emotive appeal rather than from a precise and detailed analysis of the causal processes involved. The case of material deprivation may illustrate this point. It has been found that a causal relationship between material advantage (such as the size of family income or the ownership of property) and achievement is generally very weak. The studies in this area, sometimes even of extreme poverty, show the overriding importance of cultural variables and the insignificance of material advantage. Svalastoga (1964), for example, found that income differences were poorly correlated with other background variables; the Crowther Report (1959) showed that 'even in the lowest income group approximately 30 per cent of children stayed at school beyond the age of 16'.

However, someone who holds to the 'material disadvantage thesis' may object that such statistical correlations and analyses do not prove anything since they may be claimed to have only misrepresented or obscured the causal mechanisms involved. The same objections can be raised for every one of the other explanations. They each are based on a set of empirical associations whose causal network is impossible to unravel. Unlike the causal association between 'bad schools' and 'dumb kids', that between 'poor parents' and 'dumb kids' is not so easily established or refuted. We may be able to expose children from different backgrounds to a controlled range of school environments, but we cannot experiment with families. Because low income, low motivation, low parental involvement and poor test scores go together, it is not possible to say which of the home environment variables is 'making the difference'.

Therefore, the claim that there is a weak causal link between low income and low scores is a very dubious inference. First, there are so many variables involved in such research that unless one has a definite causal theory of the priority of one variable over another, it is impossible to eliminate any one by statistical analysis alone. We could not be sure, in other words, whether it was low income that was causing low parental interest and it was low parental interest that was causing low scores. If this were so, then the 'partial' relationship between income and scores would be weak even though its *causal* relationship is of prime importance. The problem of choosing between a number of simultaneous predictors bedevils the exploration of causal mechanisms in these family background studies.

Underlying this problem is the fact that in the absence of any well accepted theory of deprivation almost any type of model may be plausibly used to arrange the variables in a causal sequence. In other words, we could rearrange the variables to fit, say, a model of cultural transmission, or material transmission, or even of 'self-fulfilling prophecy', but we could not establish which was the correct one. Any field that seems to be so poorly understood is, therefore, hardly ready for policy. There have been many attempts to isolate the factors of deprivation, but the boundaries between science and ideology, as Baratz and Baratz (1970) show, are difficult to discern. Until either different methods of study are employed or more testable propositions are suggested, it would seem that the vast amount of findings accumulated on family background will never provide the basis for understanding the cultural mechanisms of scholastic achievement.

2 *Social background and educational attainment*

In tracing the links between background and credentials we go one step further along the life cycle. Here at least we may be on slightly firmer ground. Perhaps if we cannot explain why children from certain backgrounds read better than others, we can give some good sound reasons why they leave school at different ages. We have already seen that the retention rate of different schools is difficult to explain and it cannot be put down simply to the allocation of resources. We have also seen that the success rates for the same kinds of children under different types of systems (selective or comprehensive) are almost identical. Having ruled out the differences in the school environment as a mechanism of transmitting privilege we have at least cleared the deck for other kinds of explanation.

Although we might think that the issues were more clear-cut here, there is nevertheless still great room for disagreement. The clearest division here is between those who see educational attainment as an extension of the process measured by tests of scholastic achievement, and those who see it as a different kind of phenomenon. We have, therefore, on the one hand, different variations of the 'culture of poverty' and 'cultural capital' and 'self-fulfilling prophecy' arguments which see the decision to 'drop out' as merely a terminal point in a whole history of individual failure, while, on the other, we have those which claim that there are distinctive mechanisms of educational choice which cannot be explained in terms of the cultural discontinuity between the home and the school.

The 'value' theory of attainment. In the first type of approach it is often claimed that different social classes put a different value on educational credentials. The working classes by and large do not see credentials in terms of personal fulfilment or even as the means of acquiring personally satisfying jobs. They are interested in tangible rewards for effort and job security even if this means low personal fulfilment. They, therefore, do not aspire very high and perceive the attainment process as a mixture of good fortune and having the right contacts. The middle classes, however, are supposed to set a relatively high value on education as a means of 'getting on'. They see it as a channel to personal satisfaction as well as material success, even if this means some degree of uncertainty. The children of the middle classes, therefore, try to attain as high as they can. This theory is outlined by Hyman (1953) and was held by a variety of theorists, mainly of liberal persuasions.

There are many difficulties with this theory and a second interpretation has consequently been developed by Keller and Zavalloni (1964). These sociologists found that there were just too many deviant cases among both middle-class and working-class children to be ignored. It was apparent that there were many working-class children who placed a high value on education for life chances, and that there were as well many middle-class children who placed a low value on education. Nevertheless, the social position of the children's fathers did have some influence on their levels of aspiration. How could this paradox be explained? Keller and Zavalloni proposed that the value that a child places on education may have to be related to where he starts in the social structure. A manual child for example who aspires to even a low-level white collar job which would require only a high school certificate may in fact be just as ambitious as a non-manual child who wants to go to college and professional school. Attainment, therefore, may not be determined by the value placed on education, but by the social 'distance' that a child has to travel to reach a particular educational or social level.

The 'social position' theory of attainment. This theory of Keller and Zavalloni is expanded by Boudon (1974) into a much more elaborate theory of attainment. This may be called the 'social position' theory as opposed to the 'value' theory of Hyman and others. Boudon examines the relationships between IQ, scholastic attainment, social background and aspirations in several contexts, from American and Danish surveys. He found that it was impossible to account for the variation of aspirations within the same social class as a function of IQ, or scholastic achievement by the 'value' theory. A student's desire to go on to college was more strongly influenced by his IQ and his school record than by his social origins. He asks: 'Indeed, can we perhaps explain the variations of level of aspiration for a given level of, say, school achievement, without introducing the notion that classes differ with respect to their system of values?'

Boudon, therefore, proposes a kind of 'two tier' theory of attainment. First there are the 'primary effects' of social background which are similar to those noted above for IQ and for school achievement. Next, we have the 'secondary effects' which apply when two children of different social backgrounds, but equal scores of IQ and scholastic achievement, have to choose between two kinds of curricula. The 'secondary effects', Boudon claims, are not to be explained simply in terms of the value of cultural systems of the social classes, but by the costs and benefits associated with each particular social level.

What are these costs and benefits? Boudon suggests that for an upper-class child, choosing a vocational course would mean social demotion. He would, therefore, be more likely to choose a course which leads to the same social status as his parents, even though this way may represent a financial cost and even if his intellectual ability is not very high. On the other hand, a working-class child would have less interest in choosing a prestigious course rather than a vocational course because he would probably have to make greater financial sacrifices, because he would have less social pressure to do so, and because the psychological tensions of leaving the social level of his family and friendship group could be considerable. Boudon concludes that the higher the social status of the family the higher the benefits and the lower the cost associated with choosing an academic curriculum over a vocational one. It is, therefore, possible to account for the differences in educational choice without supposing that working-class families place a lower value on educational attainment or do not see the connection between credentials and jobs.

A theory of educational choice

There is one very promising approach which appears to arise directly out of Boudon's 'social position' theory. This is the theory of educational choice formulated by Lane (1972). It is an approach which attempts to demonstrate how differences in economic circumstances are translated into educational attainment.

Lane offers an economic explanation of educational choice not in terms of the size of parents' income, but in terms of what he calls 'income career'. This is the pattern of earnings of the father over time. On this it is claimed, the child constructs his 'model of the world' and consequently derives the value of having a certain credential. Whether or not an extra year of education is perceived as useful is then not related primarily to the father's economic well-being, but rather to the cultural orientations of the home based on the stability and predictability of his income. This is not the same thing either as 'social status' since it is possible to enjoy different 'income careers' within the same broad status level. It may be possible then to use this concept to account for the differences in values and cultural influences of the home in economic terms.

This concept of 'income career' may perhaps be linked to a

'social position' theory to arrive at a rather tighter explanation of educational choice than has been so far presented. This is because Lane may have identified a common source of both 'primary' or cultural effects and of 'secondary' or 'positional' effects, in terms of Boudon's model of choice described above. The parents' 'income career' may be the basis of the cultural variables associated with achievement and aspirations. In addition, it may set precise limits on the costs and benefits of moving up one more rung of the educational ladder. These costs and benefits may be economic, since a more unstable, unpredictable income would be a rather unsteady basis for sending a child to university. These may also be psychological, since the decision to take an extra year's education may mean leaving the income patterns of one's own family and peer group for a 'better' life style – the difference that an 'O' level certificate can make between the assembly-line and the office staff.

A study of the distribution of these costs of educational choice for families grouped by industry, region, consumption level and so on might tell us more about the patterns of demand for academic curricula. It may also tell us what are the crucial factors in the decision to drop out. These factors may be identified as unique combinations of any one of these variables with different degrees of income stability and predictability. Such an analysis could possibly fill out the great gaps in our present knowledge of educational attainment, particularly of the 'secondary' effects of social background which would seem to be more accessible to intervention than are the 'primary' effects on intelligence and school achievement. It may appear, for example, that many of the variations in educational attainment noted by Byrne, Williamson and Fletcher could be better explained in these terms rather than in the provision of certain kinds of courses and facilities. This is only a tentative suggestion at this stage, but in the absence of more fruitful lines of enquiry, it needs to be considered.

It appears then that we are back in the world of labour markets, educational upgrading and social mobility that was discussed in Chapter 2. There is some basis now for bringing together the findings on educational and scholastic outcomes into a rounded picture of the intergenerational transmission of status. As we have seen, this is a necessary step since the decision to take another year of education is influenced not only by the positions of the father or his 'income career', but by the anticipation that more education will lead to social mobility. The wrench that education may imply in social terms cannot be ignored in counting the costs of an extra year of schooling. These status expectations from extra schooling may vary from region to region, from level to level and from time to time.

3 Social background and mobility

How much can a working-class child really hope to gain socially from having a higher educational level than his father? The 'liberal' answer is: Quite a lot.' Irrespective of the father's status, it will be claimed that a boy who works hard and goes to college can expect to gain a much higher status and income than his father. This liberal belief was well exemplified in the movie *Guess Who's Coming to Dinner*, where a well-qualified black was confronted by the latent prejudice of a white middle-class family. The issue at stake was: If all other things are equal, do ethnic origins still count in a liberal democracy? This is an insincere question in many ways since in the real world 'other things' are rarely equal – few blacks in the US, for example, achieve the distinction of the young doctor played by Sidney Poitier in this film. We are back then to the thorny old question as to whether education only reinforces family background or whether it acts as an independent agent of social ascent.

One of the earliest post-war challenges to the 'liberal' view came from an empirical study of mobility in three countries (US, Sweden and Britain) by Anderson (1961). This study showed that in every country there were many sons who had a lower social position than their fathers even though their education level was higher. Conversely, many sons had attained a status that was equal to that of their fathers even though they were not as well educated. In fact, if we were to draw up two hypothetical tables, one in which we assumed that relative education had a maximum effect on relative status, and one where we assume that relative education has no effect on relative status, we would find that it is the *latter* which is far closer to empirical reality. Despite the fact that Anderson's data were excellent and that the finding applied to all three countries, this paper made very little impact on the policies of the 1960s which continued to operate under the liberal assumption.

One explanation of Anderson's findings might be that educational attainment is not important anyway for social mobility.

This is not because, as in the 'class conflict' model, it is only a screening device for eliminating those with the 'wrong' background, but because there is *always* a high probability of social ascent or descent whatever the level of a son's educational attainment. This is in fact the explanation provided by Boudon (1974) who claims that a large amount of mobility will take place despite (a) the bias of the educational system in favour of the middle-class child and (b) the fact that the hiring process gives more qualified applicants 'an edge' over the others. Since children of all classes have to pass through the 'filters' of schooling and the labour market, the chances of promotion for the children of low social origins and of demotion for those of high origins are always likely to be considerable. We will come back to Boudon's model after the next section.

Education and social mobility in Britain

It should be possible to test which of these explanations is the more plausible for a country like Britain, and to ascertain whether there is in fact a low correlation between education and mobility in this country. On the one hand, we could put forward a 'class conflict' hypothesis, on the other a kind of 'Jencksian' hypothesis where individual randomness is the dominant force. This is not exactly 'luck', however, because the process may itself be quite well understood. Is there any clear basis for choosing between the two?

Those who hold a 'class conflict' view, that education is only a kind of 'cover' for existing privilege, might be encouraged at the evidence of the determinants of the incomes of social scientists (Westoby, Webster and Williams, 1976). This study looked at the relationships between the incomes of more than a thousand graduates in the social sciences in 1972, and their educational, social and individual characteristics. They found that there were superficial associations between the type of school and university attended but that when social and personal variables (age, sex) were controlled for, these associations tended to disappear. Although past pupils of independent schools earned £623 more than those from grammar schools, when their other advantages and subsequent occupations were controlled for, this difference dropped to only £85. By contrast the effect of the duration of the father's education remained fairly constant when other factors like class of degree, university and school and personal variables were allowed for. The 'drop' here was quite small – from £1,449 to £836. These findings confirm what was said about the 'Balliol man' at the beginning of Chapter 3 and may also shed some light on the processes of status inheritance.

A detailed answer to the relative importance of social background, education and ability in the status attainment process must wait until a further study and analysis has been carried out. However, from the discussion in Chapter 3 which showed a remarkable degree of similarity between the patterns of educational ascent in the United States and in Britain and from the path diagram in the Appendix to Chapter 4, it would appear that a 'Jencks-type' model would apply to this country quite well. In other words, while there appears to be a fairly high relationship between education and occupational status, a moderate relationship between education and social background and a rather weak relationship between social background and occupational status, the whole process of status attainment is open to a huge amount of 'chance'. Education may act both as a conveyor-belt of privilege and as a promoter of ability but there appears always to be a good deal of randomness in the way that individuals are eventually sorted into the hierarchy of occupations.

Deciding just how much of the relationship between educational attainment and rewards is essentially 'reproductive' depends mainly on one's perspective. One might say that, because of the openness of the occupational system, we have almost arrived at a point of maximum fairness. This is the conclusion of Treiman and Terrell (1975:577) who claim that in both Britain and in the US 'education is largely independent of social origins and thus serves mainly as a channel of social mobility rather than as an instrument of status maintenance'. This view must, however, be put alongside the finding of Ridge (1974:41) that in Britain in the first part of this century about a third of the amount of status inheritance that takes place is carried through education. One might be surprised to learn moreover that the 'facts' are not in dispute here, since the relationships observed by Treiman and Terrell and those of Ridge's analysis are not widely different. It appears to be mainly a question of whether one is looking at the whole attainment process, in which education is definitely a facilitator of upward mobility, or whether one is looking at its role within the cycles of privilege or disadvantage that exist, however small these may be. Here its influence is both constant and powerful.

The analysis of Ridge is particularly relevant in helping us to focus on this 'paradox' of educational ascent:

> The evidence supports only a weak hypothesis on the 'tightening links' between education and occupation in this period (roughly the first half of the century). Adult occupation becomes more dependent on the level of educational attainment at several stages; at the secondary stage the importance of the Ordinary School Certificate examination increases sharply, and at the post-school stage formal qualifications become more relevant. But the overall effect is if anything to increase the correlation of father's and son's status (that is, to reduce the amount of status mobility between generations): this seems to be due in part to the increased dependence of educational attainment on social origin (father's status). Within the education process itself, the differences between types of secondary school become much more consequential, especially for success in the School Certificate competition. Entry into further education becomes, in a limited sense, more open: the School Certificate is less necessary, but the influence of the secondary school itself increases. Access to qualifications does appear genuinely more open, through routes other than formal further education; but although occupational status becomes more dependent on qualifications, the effect is not great enough to produce any increase in status-mobility between fathers and sons.

In many ways this finding is not unlike the other 'paradox' met in Chapter 2, where the escalator image was used to describe the stable relationship between education and jobs. As rising levels of educational attainment are accepted for occupational entry, there is an apparent increase in the demand for skill and talent, unconnected with social origin. In some respects this is true, since each cohort of young people must compete for higher levels of qualification, and the upper echelons are open to a rather randomly distributed ability. However, such a tendency, as the French Marxists Bourdieu and Passeron (1970) tell us, also defends the interests of the privileged through the hidden processes of cultural transmission (see Kennet, 1973). It must be pointed out, however, that while, as Ridge shows, the compensations within the reproductive 'machine' rule out any significant increase in social opportunity, status inheritance has not *increased* over the century. In other words, the 'luck of the race' has *not* succumbed to attempts to rationalize the process of status transmission under the guise of formal schooling and meritocratic selection.

For a full understanding of the role of education we appear to need an explanation that has more complexity than any of the models discussed so far and outlined in Chapter 1, since it is not simply a question of education 'reproducing' class relationships, any more than it is of modern democracies being 'open' to talent of all social origins. Both of these approaches give an inadequate view, even though one may find a good deal of evidence for each taken separately.

Boudon and the 'luck' factor

In order to understand the mobility process we have to turn to a model such as that outlined by Boudon. This model, based on a 'fictitious' society, demonstrates how it is possible to generate a large degree of randomness in a society that is characterized both by a strong class bias in attainment and a strong credentialist bias in the labour market. The randomness is not like Jencks' 'luck' factor, but is rather an outcome of systematic tendencies in the process itself. To use a gaming analogy, Boudon tries to understand the mechanisms of the 'fruit-machine', whereas Jencks is content merely to analyse the payout sequences.

How does the model that Boudon presents actually work? It is perhaps futile to try to capture here all of the complexity of this model, but the principles may be stated quite simply. At the heart of both educational and occupational attainment there is a competition for the best places and the best jobs. However, in this 'race' there are handicaps. Individual children of the privileged are more likely to get the favoured school places and qualifications, but there is no guarantee that they will. Similarly, the labour market favours, but does not always select, applicants with the best credentials. Thirdly, and probably most important of all, there is no necessary agreement between the number of people with credentials being produced by the schools and the demands of the labour market. Because of this there is usually a competition for jobs among equally well-qualified applicants; the children of high social backgrounds, although relatively more numerous among the best qualified, often have to be satisfied with a less prestigious position than that of their fathers.

The combination of the two 'hurdles' brings about a good deal of rather arbitrary resorting and hence of a rather stable amount of social mobility. Even with very high 'handicaps' (80 per cent and 70 per cent), against children with low social class and poor credentials, Boudon shows that a large number of high status children will experience demotion, and a large number of low status children will be promoted. Out of 320 'top' children in social and educational background in his first model, only 92 reach the status of their parents; out of 5077 of those from bottom families in status and educational levels, 1903 reach the next highest status, and 95 climb to the top status group. This model seems to fit the picture of mobility in most industrialized societies. Certainly it seems to fit the tables of mobility in British society while providing a more satisfactory explanation of 'luck' than has been given so far. Indeed, Boudon's model goes a long way towards explaining (1) why there is such a degree of apparent randomness in the occupational attainment process (2) why education does not seem to affect social mobility and (3) why, despite the great expansion in average educational attainment, the patterns of social ascent remain very stable across the generations.

We have apparently come a long way from the original image of the steeple chase – or have we? Could we not still think of the social ascent as a kind of race and look at each step of the educational ladder as a kind of obstacle? At some obstacles 'weight' is more important than starting position and form, at others it is the reverse. At no stage, however, is it possible to be certain that any one contestant will survive, even though everything may be going in his favour. The final outcome is not determinate, even though the system of handicapping may be. If the outcome of the race determines entrance to another class or division and the places there are relatively few, then individual chances are even more uncertain. Changing the conditions of the events, the structure of the course or the system of handicaps will not, of course, make the race any more predictable. Although no-one yet has found how to make it more 'fair' we must not turn away from this task. Indeed, it is just possible that the findings presented in the foregoing chapters may enable us to provide some new insights into educational policy.

6

Fairness and merit: a reappraisal of educational policy

Why do some children read so badly and get such poor school grades? Why do they leave school at sixteen? Why can't they get jobs? These are considered to be among the most important social questions of today and yet no-one can answer them satisfactorily. As argued in this book, the reason why they remain unanswered is that the approaches of sociologists, educators and politicians have been wildly unscientific. Instead of looking at inequality as a barely understood system, they have tried to explain everything by a single determinant. Each of the first five models presented in Chapter 1 have, one way and another, relied on a single origin of inequality – whether it be in privileged backgrounds, in school quality or organization, in IQ genotype or in credentials. This is not the way to attack the problem, since inequality is multi-causal.

In addition to focusing on a single explanation, these models have failed because they relate only to separate individuals and not to the over-arching structures and the greater institutions of society. This has led to a rather spurious emphasis on randomness or 'luck'. Of these institutions the one that theorists have said most about – namely the educational system itself – is the one that probably matters the least. It is perhaps time then that educational inequality could be appreciated in its full complexity. This complexity appears to be produced by the very nature of industrial society – in the supply and demand for educated labour, in the costs and benefits of extra schooling and in the many interfaces between social background, schooling and the reward structure that lead inexorably to a large component of individual randomness.

One of the first propositions of this book was that any statement about one of the dimensions of inequality usually implied a theory of the interconnections between all six. It may follow then that the theoretical and practical inadequacy of all of the models we have examined means that the components that went into the model – that is the dimensions themselves – need to be looked at again. Are these six variables the *only* analytical elements of a model of educational inequality or do we need perhaps to replace them with a totally new set that may do justice to both the complexity and the structural origins of the concept? I believe we do. Not only might a new set of dimensions form the basis for a new theoretical approach, they may also provide an orientation for educators of all kinds to reappraise their day-to-day policies and procedures.

What could these new dimensions be? The socio-economic orientation of the approach taken so far should not blind us to the philosophical dimension. It would be helpful if we could unite all of the rather dry analytic concepts of a new model of educational inequality with a firm defining principle. Again, what could this be? Let us begin with the proposition that education – in attainment, in access, in provision and in its contribution to life chances – is a social 'good'. This is to say that most people would rather be educated than not. If this is so, what principle should guide its distribution? At present the distribution of all of the six dimensions of educational inequality tends to be isomorphous with the distribution of most other 'goods' – of power and wealth and services, whether individually or institutionally defined. Are we to accept before starting then the inherent justice of the present educational and social structure of industrial society? For a fresh model we need a fresh definition of social justice and for this we turn to the philosophy of Rawls (1971) whose 'difference principle' provides a radical and yet reformist approach to the distribution of social rewards.

The 'social pie' and the 'difference principle'

Justice, according to Rawls, concerns rules for distributing socially valued goods and services. It is based on the principle of fairness that governs natural situations. If, for example, five people have to share an asset (say, a pie, or a piece of land), if none of the people have a special right, then the rule must be that each should obtain an equal share. Justice, fairness and equality are, therefore, inseparable in this concrete example. However, complex societies do not always present such explicit opportunities for applying the rule of fairness. If inequalities arise, as they seem to in every society, what then should be the guiding rule? This is the most novel part of Rawls' theory for it is here that he introduces the 'difference principle' which stands the conventional liberal and meritocratic notion of inequality on its head. The social ideal according to Rawls (1971 : 303) is that 'All social primary goods – liberty and opportunity, income and wealth; and the bases of self-respect – are to be distributed equally unless an unequal distribution of any or all of these goods is to the advantage of the least favoured.'

The 'evolutionary liberal' and the 'meritocratic' models are, therefore, rejected since they attempt to establish a natural aristocracy which is based on undeserved endowments, be they from social or biological inheritance or from good fortune. Neither is the answer to be found in tinkering with an unfair system, as dictated by the 'compensatory' model. The aim of Rawls is to equalize not opportunity but results or outcomes. As Bell (1972) points out in a comment on Rawls, this betokens the end of liberalism. Halsey (1975a), a chief exponent of Rawls' ideas in Britain, goes further and sees in them the making of the 'new socialist philosophy'. The logic of the present distribution of social goods which follows the principle of 'first come first served' may then be basically unfair. The Darwinist elements in the liberal model appear to guide us to the wrong dimensions of inequality – i.e. to those that can probably never be changed even by the most extreme forms of intervention.

The 'difference principle' has two aspects of relevance to policy. The main one is the principle of 'redress' for individuals who are disadvantaged. In this connection Rawls suggests that greater resources might be spent on the education of the less rather than the more intelligent, at least over a certain time of life, say, the earlier years of school. This is obviously similar to a compensatory model but it is derived from a principle of fairness that regards education as 'good' in its own right, not as an instrument of social engineering. The poor have a right to more education because they have less of everything else. The second implication for social policy is that talents are to be defined as a 'common asset'. All are to share equally (or unequally in the positive discriminatory sense) in its fruits. The marginal productivity, if any, of educated labour should, therefore, not be used to buy more inequality, as appears now to be the case. Equality of opportunity should produce equal benefits, both social and individual.

Education, both as a 'good' in itself and in its effects on the welfare and the wealth of a society, should according to Rawls be distributed according to the principle of inequality in favour of the *least* advantaged. The main pitfall of applying the 'difference principle' would seem, however, to be the belief that the desirability of educational consumption is universally recognized. It is just possible that education is not to everybody's taste. The principle of 'redress' would not therefore directly apply unless one were to apply compulsion in a manner which was inconsistent with liberal principles. The answer could reside in equalizing the *choice* to continue with education rather than in directly equalizing provision or consumption.

In this regard, the potential of compensatory educational spending for redistribution is not likely to be great. In Chapter 2, for example, we examined the effects of educational expansion on the income share of the lower paid and found that over the past century there was not much diminution of this aspect of inequality. Massive expenditure aimed at equalizing the consumption of education in these 'raw' terms would not be the way to equalizing incomes.

However, within the present arrangements, certain inequities appear that may explain the weak impact of educational spending. The most important of these appears to be the take-up of university places by the different social groups. As Glennerster (1972) points out, those in the lowest social class group (unskilled workers) pay one fifth as much tax as those in the highest (professionals), but have only one seventeenth the chance of having a son or daughter at university. Although this latter figure could perhaps be modified downwards a little in the light of later research (Halsey, 1975b), there are certainly many areas of educational expenditure where adjustments, however slight in their total redistributive effects, could be made.

The moves in this direction – either in 'squeezing' the universities to build nursery schools or in applying 'quota' schemes to university places for the poor – need to be looked at again. On the one hand, as we have seen in Chapter 3, there is very little evidence that reallocation of resources will have radical effects on learning. If this is the case, it may be a disservice to working-class children to cut back on those institutions where education, in terms of individual returns at least, offers them the potentially highest pay-offs. On the other hand, the enforcement of 'quota' schemes may have the same effect as the raising of the school leaving age, by devaluing the currency without altering the underlying pattern of inequality.

There are, of course, other considerations beside those of fairness and equality. Some of the other social goals that need to inform policy are no less important: practicality, liberty and efficiency. These may be highly interdependent. In the following redefinition of educational inequality these have been taken into account to produce social indices that can be immediately incorporated into public debate and perhaps into policy. These will revolve around three topics; consumption, outcomes and returns. In Rawls' terms, the first two concern the principle of 'redress' and will be dealt with together, while the last concerns redistribution of the productions of talent.

Inequities in division and outcome

For the following discussion I rely heavily on an article by Mary Jean Bowman on the economic perspectives of education and 'life opportunities'. This article highlights most of the issues touched on here, though not from a Rawlsian perspective. Basically, the problem of equity revolves around the choice of a strategy of provision (in the broad sense), since this is the area where policy can be most effective. Bowman (1975: 74) gives seven definitions of equity in the provision of education, few of which, she remarks, were made by economists:

1 Giving equal amounts of schooling (equal schooling inputs) to every individual.

2 Bringing every individual to a stipulated minimum level of performance, whatever happens thereafter.
3 Bringing every individual to the same level of performance.
4 Ensuring that each individual receives the schooling that will enable him to realize his full potentialities.
5 Bringing each individual to the point at which his marginal ratio of added learning to inputs matches that for other individuals.
6 Providing equal opportunity for access to education whether individuals utilize that opportunity or not.
7 Ensuring proportional representation from every ethnic, social status, sex and other relevant category of individuals.

These seven definitions will guide the following discussion.

The first has been the traditional goal of liberal policy in the first part of this century, within the limits of a statutory leaving age. Successful as it may have been, such a policy has not eliminated the fairly obvious bias in outcomes. We saw in Chapter 3 that the greatest source of variation in outcomes was not the quality of resources or inputs. These, in fact, were remarkably similar within administrative areas and did not account, as had been thought, for the low achievement of 'inner-ring' or 'downtown' schools. Opportunity is not definable in terms of resources, even though one may feel that they have the greatest claim, under the principle of equity. If one stops at resources or inputs, or even if one advocates an extreme policy of compensatory opportunity, the equalization of performance will not be attained.

There is nothing, of course, preventing policy-makers from accepting this and at the same time applying the 'difference principle' to its full. Redress in the form of provision is in fact one of the positive recommendations of Jencks. As he claims, 'There is no evidence that building a school playground, for example, will affect students' chances of learning to read, getting into college, or making $50,000 a year when they are 50. Building a playground may, however, have a considerable effect on the students' chances of having a good time during recess when they are 8' (1972:29). It is very doubtful, however, whether the wholehearted search for equity in this area would be the most desirable way of reversing any present inequities in public expenditure or in equalizing personal costs. Apart from dramatically reducing visible inequality it would probably have little more than a cosmetic and rather short term advantage.

The second, third and fourth proposals, as Bowman notes, attempt to reverse the resources aspect and concentrate on outcomes without reference to costs. She calls the second (equality of minimum performance) the 'sanest and also the most incomplete' – with which it is hard to disagree. The third proposal she regards as fanciful and points out that equalized achievement would require halting learning by the most energetic and enthusiastic individuals until others caught up. We simply do not know how to produce equality short of some horrendous policy of negative discrimination against the able. The impact of educational treatments as against individual differences, motivation, ability and other personality traits will always be slight. The fourth definition ('realization of full potentialities') is, I suspect, speech night rhetoric or else a dubious gloss on the class differential in outcomes.

The fifth proposal presents an interesting angle on the problems of provision. It means that additional resources would be allocated to a person's schooling as long as such an allocation yielded results, in relative terms. If, as would seem to be the case, the more able were better able to exploit their inputs at each investment level, then, as Bowman points out, this would have a meritocratic criterion. On the other hand, if the less able were more sensitive in certain areas to better teaching, then they would have a greater claim to the additional resources. Within the narrow margins of schooling effects mentioned above, this proposal has certain advantages. A good compensatory case could be made here, but it would have to be 'treatment specific' or 'cost-effective'. The difficulty here is that those precise treatment variations that do make the difference in achievement or attainment are very difficult to pin down.

In general, however, this proposal contains the germs of an equitable policy. It may even be further modified to include a redistributive element. That is to say, a scale of 'objective' disadvantage could be used in conjunction with the marginal learning returns to produce something like an agreed index of priority. There are obvious limits to how much one can apply the distributive principle without falling into the vortex of compensation for its own sake. Such an index, however, may allow policy-makers to combine the most promising developments in pedagogy with the notion of fairness.

Let us go ahead a little and turn to the seventh definition (equalizing group outcomes) which is popular with many reformers who follow the Rawlsian position. It implies, in many interpretations, the imposition of quotas to ensure that there is rough equity in the distribution of college or university places. As Bowman suggests, this is at best a 'transitional' measure whose main utility would be as a strategy of shock in attacking entrenched discrimination. The use of quotas is perhaps justifiable in this short-term context, but it leads to violations of that other universal principle – civil liberty. In attempting to break down the discrimination of educational practice it necessarily involves particularistic or ascriptive criteria that are difficult to justify in legal or constitutional terms. Even in educational terms the end result could be the institutionalization of closed and mutually repressive ideologies.

This 'hard' version of equity of a quota system would impose stresses that are incompatible not simply with liberty but probably with efficiency as well. It should be recalled that the logic of functionalism was dictated by a code of honour or prestige that attempted to reconcile rewards with merit. It is not surprising that the demise of the functionalist paradigm should see the rise of a distributive system which sees earned status as arbitrary or as irrational as the ascriptive qualities of ethnicity or sex. The decline of 'honour' as a modern code of identity and the rise of 'dignity' described by Berger *et al.* (1973) is seen in an extreme form in the imposition of quotas. However, as Runciman (1967) points out, while all men are entitled to respect, they are not all entitled to praise. To ignore or override differences in competence or ability is to endanger the quality of institutional life and ultimately perhaps to commit another injustice.

Is it possible, however, to maintain some element of reward for merit and still aspire to equality of group outcomes? This is the aim of Halsey, who prescribes interventionist and gradualist methods. Halsey locates the origins of inequality of educational outcomes in communal and work situations rather than in individuals or in schools. According to this argument then, it is not too much to expect that eventually 'non-educationally defined groups' should have proportionate representation at, say, Oxford and Cambridge. This application of the Rawlsian principle is, however, perceived as a threat to the variety of English culture by Robert Jackson (1972–3), whose running debate with Halsey makes fascinating reading. According to Jackson, the very notion of state-planned egalitarianism necessarily diminishes individual and local liberties and hence the quality of life.

However one places oneself in this debate, the wisdom and the feasibility of compensatory opportunity needs further examination. If we are to aim at educational equity, is the 'representational' ideal a desirable one? I believe not, for two main reasons: (a) on the technical side it is possible to demonstrate the probable inefficacy of all engineering approaches, as discussed in Chapter 3; (b) from a philosophical point of view the emphasis on equalization of result implies a paternalism that ignores the realities of culturally and economically defined choice. Whether one agrees with Jackson that such diversity is desirable, one cannot deny that it acts as a powerful constraint. Who, indeed, is to decide between 'Shakespeare and Manchester United'? Therefore, concentrating mechanistically on the equalization of group results may be an unprofitable distraction from the flexibility gained by a more imaginative approach to the problem of opportunity. It is in this regard that we turn to the sixth proposal enumerated by Bowman, which depends upon a model of educational choice.

A socio-economic approach to opportunity

If equalizing opportunity cannot be tested against the facile criteria of equalization of group outcomes the question then revolves around the mechanism of rationing – what is to be rationed and how. In the model of status attainment the most central educational variable is formal attainment. The role of cognitive skills and type of schooling is to distribute access to credentials which are then 'cashed in' on life chances. What we need is some mechanism which would ensure that the able or affluent are not deterred from attaining while ensuring that the less able or the poor are given every encouragement. Such a mechanism will have to be sensitive to the total returns, both individual and social, on educational investment. Leaving aside this issue of returns for the moment, however, we will concentrate on the short-term costs and benefits of an extra year of education.

A model of educational choice

The simplest approach to educational choice would stem from the fact that the financial cost of an extra year's education is greater for a poor person than it is for a rich person. Such an approach to educational choice could lead, under the general principle of equity, to the transfer of wealth via the taxation system to redistribute costs more fairly. Under the principle of redress it may entail actually paying children from poor homes to stay on at school. However, we need to consider whether determinants of choice are purely economic or a combination of economic and sociological factors that both need to be considered before a workable definition of opportunity can be put forward.

This is the problem addressed by Raymond Boudon (1974, 1975). Dissatisfied with the culturalist theory of traditional sociology of education, as well as with the purely economic theory outlined above, Boudon (as we saw in Chapter 5) develops what may be called a 'structural' or 'social position' theory of educational choice that relies both on the cultural constraints on the individual and his family as well as on the different costs and benefits of staying on at school. This theory also incorporates the element of ability and motivation in that previous educational achievement also acts as a constraint on the decision to take another year's schooling. The main advantage of this theory is that it is possible to include those cultural constraints that are specific to an individual's region, social background or peer group. As we saw in the examination of Lane's concept of 'income career' in Chapter 5, these cultural orientations may also have an economic and structural basis.

Put simply, this approach of Boudon proposes that the social origin of the student adds to or subtracts from the utility of 'staying on' at school. This is not the same as the blanket culturalist statement 'that working-class children value education less than middle-class children', which is moreover contradicted by the evidence. Rather it states that the stratification of opportunities is determined largely by the costs and benefits of surpassing the social position of the father. To middle-class families the cost of a prestigious education may be less than the benefits if 'all the others' are doing the same. By the same token, a small objective effort to better one's educational position may be enormously costly in psychological terms if it will alienate the student from his social origins.

What are the implications of this for policy? A fiscal transfer from the rich to the poor to encourage them to stay on at school may not adequately subsidize the costs involved. Exactly how great these costs and benefits are, is, of course, extremely difficult to determine. It is fairly obvious that a simple equalization of financial costs by tax relief will not be sufficient. In this regard the French 'family quotient system' as noted by Eicher and Mingat (1975) has apparently only a slight redistributive effect. There has to be either an extreme shift towards redressive, as against compensatory, opportunity at the fiscal level or else some mechanism for broadening the horizons set by the family from which the non-economic costs are determined.

Here at least, in the area of educational choice, there is still a great deal that could be done. Bowman lists some of the possibilities: (a) 'pooled' financing of all public service costs where provision would be governed by consumer preference; (b) levelling of wealth or income of the whole population of families; (c) improving the 'capital markets' for investments in schooling. This last possibility has several models, such as the use of full-cost tuition, adjustable loan schemes, and the like.

One could add to Bowman's list the 'voucher' system which has already been tried in the USA. In the simpler version of this system a 'voucher' representing the average cost of education for each child is given to the family to be cashed in at the school of choice, though different compensatory devices are possible (Maynard, 1975). This approach is very appealing to the liberal conscience but has the basic flaw that it does not really equalize access to credentials but rather to school environments. In the light of the previous discussion on the weak causal effect of school environments this is a false option. Despite its potential for expanding consumer choice the compensatory mechanisms built into these schemes would only make it easier for the poor to 'buy' the education they may now receive as a social service. Even if the vouchers did give them access to 'better' environments that are now outside their grasp, it is highly likely that these would do little to enhance *either* their educational attainment *or* their life chances. Although these schemes, including those mentioned by Bowman, have the germs of redistributive justice, they represent at present only directions of attack that need to be more fully reconnoitred.

The major constraints on equalizing access to credentials, as we have seen, originate outside the school system. Compulsion in the form of raising the school leaving age does not equalize opportunity and we could not expect any similarly coercive scheme, universally applied, to give anything more than bureaucratic consolation. Moreover, any denial of opportunity to the brightest, though similarly egalitarian, may be in the real sense of the word, counter-productive. On the other hand, making educational attainment a mere matter of consumer choice would be an act of indiscriminate liberalism, since it would almost certainly benefit those who were already well poised in the social race. Any move towards 'deschooling' would be similarly unfair. What is obviously needed is a compromise between compulsion and extreme liberalism.

While 'voucher' schemes should be rejected for their preoccupation with increasing the choice of school environments, they may yet contain some features that would inform a policy of equalizing costs of 'staying-on'. Certain vouchers, for example, offer the possibility of relating educational expenditure to family income. While these have been proposed as a means of raising the educational purchasing power of low-income families, there is no apparent reason why they should not be geared to the *duration* rather than to the *type* of schooling that children receive.

Of particular interest here for policy would be the interplay between sociological dimensions of family background (size, status and other attributes) and the estimates of costs and benefits. Since unravelling the specific problems of school survival depends on an understanding of the social as well as of the economic costs, it is possible that the general parameters of attainment (e.g. from a path model) could be of considerable value. Further study may show that this area of the 'secondary' effects of the home is more susceptible to direct intervention than have been the 'primary' effects on achievement and ability. Such an analysis would, however, be incomplete without a consideration not only of the costs and benefits of extra education to the family but also its lifetime returns both to the individual and to society.

Equity and the returns on education

Who should benefit from educational success? If the poorest segments of the community succeed least in the schools and gain least from their success in added earning power, how can one then justify the practice of educational stratification? We looked at this question in Chapter 2 and saw that the 'investment in human beings' school of economic thought, as well as those who adhere to what Thurow called the 'wage competition' model, attempt to do just this. The link between education and rewards, it is claimed, benefits everybody. The workers who become more productive raise the general standard of living and contribute more to national income and so enhance the prospects of the lower paid. From the sociological perspective, 'structural-functionalist' theory (Davis and Moore, 1945), attempts to justify the present distribution of income and status on the basis of the superior contribution of the able and/or educated individual. These theories are designed to justify the obvious fact that the more lucrative forms of educational consumption are largely supported by those who benefit from it least. One can, therefore, legitimately ask whether (a) the social returns justify the inegalitarian funding of higher education and (b) the distribution of its individual returns are in accordance with the principle of fairness, and if not, how can it be made so?

Let us look first at the cost of educating a university graduate in Britain. This has been estimated by Merrett (1975), taking into account capital costs, earnings and taxes foregone, at about £10,000 at 1972 price. If one includes the costs of support from parents and earnings foregone, the total cost was nearer to £15,000. What are the returns on this outlay? Merrett estimates average returns of less than seven per cent (after allowing for inflation) are achieved by the additional earnings of the university educated. The social returns in the shape of additional taxes received back into the community, Merrett claims, are negative, since only a fraction of the £10,000 paid out is ever retrieved. The other social or public benefits are difficult to estimate since, like 'cultural' level, general productivity and the like, they are often impossible to quantify. Obviously the balance between social and individual returns is an important constraint on any redistributive policy.

However, the common attempt to separate social from individual benefits leads to what Bowman sees as the 'fallacy that lies in the notion that there is an inherent conflict between egalitarian and allocative goals'. The issue is often stated in terms of a stark conflict between the goal of excellence on the one hand and the goal of equality on the other. The fallacy in this debate, according to Bowman, lies in the failure to distinguish between 'gains in productivity that accrue to the individuals and spillover effects in "public benefits" to the society at large'. We have seen above how difficult it is to make out a case that the social benefits of education are best pursued by allowing able individuals to raise their earnings. It does not follow, however, according to Bowman, that there is not a good deal of *public* pay off in reallocating resources to the lower levels of the system. What they may be at the 'lower levels' is difficult to assess, but such a policy of reallocating resources is not inimical to the goal of productivity.

In this connection, Layard (1974) has devised a formula for comparing the effects on 'equality' (life-time income distribution) as against 'efficiency' (contribution to national income) of allocating grants at various levels of the system. From this formula he estimates the returns on giving, say, an extra £300 per year to 16+ secondary students in education as against those in higher education. It would appear from this analysis that the most desirable policy (considering both equality and efficiency) would be one that encouraged school leavers to stay on into the sixth form. If one links this conclusion to the model of educational choice, it would seem that some form of grant (or 'voucher') that is tied to educational survival at the school level would perhaps result in greater fairness in the distribution of the immediate and the long term benefits of educational expenditure.

We have arrived then at a point where the equalization of opportunity may be reconciled with the goals of freedom and efficiency. For the more able and the privileged the incentive to go on is built into the present rewards structure, both in schooling itself and in life-time earnings. For the less able and the underprivileged one may propose incentives which redress the inequities in attainment, may offer greater opportunity, while at the same time avoid paternalism or compulsion. In each case the inequities are relieved with little damage to the other social virtues. Since every student should be confronted at the end of the year with a real choice, the total effect should be redistributive. In the light of this discussion the policies apparently pursued by British socialists in diverting resources from privileged to under-privileged sections of education do follow this logic of redistribution. They are, however, misdirected since the mere reallocation of resources into new buildings and better teaching will not buy more long term equality. If these funds were directed into strategies that equalized *use* rather than *provision*, they would stand a far greater chance of redressing the present inequities in the cost and rewards of educational attainment, and may in the long run reshape the structure of opportunity.

New indicators for educational policy

We return then to the original problem, that of redefining the basic dimensions of inequality. These may serve to relocate any debate outside the 'natural' categories of background, merit and attainment which have proven to be the building blocks of the rather sterile approaches of the past. Since concepts are the tools of theory it is hoped that the debate will thereby be oriented away from the concepts and models of Chapter 1 towards policies through which the real abuses and inequities of present arrangements can be both identified and realistically attacked.

The basic principles of these indicators are not difficult to deduce from the foregoing discussion. Where the 'natural' models of Chapter 1 posited inequality of ability or background, the new policy puts forward *redress* for these disadvantages. Where the current policy of opportunity is based on inequalities in resources and public provision, the one put forward is based on equality of individual *costs* and *benefits*. On the other hand, the emphasis on inequality of individual returns is replaced by a concern for *social* returns as measured by the benefits that accrue to all groups. It may therefore be possible to devise new social indices of educational inequality.

1 As a modest beginning, instead of proposing the equal representation of all 'non-educationally defined groups' in higher education one may suggest measures of levels of minimum performance in basic skills, such as literacy and numeracy. These need not be related to age, which would only emphasize the famous 'gaps' of the past, but would apply only at the statutory age or beyond. One would hope that the literacy rate, for example, across class, ethnic and regional groups could be

equalized within a target period. This at least is achievable, with present methods and technologies.

2 The next index is based on the reallocation of teaching resources that have a demonstrable effect (and there may not be many) according to a compensatory formula. It harnesses the equalization of the cost-effectiveness of teaching methods to the 'difference principle'. Once it was found that additional resources produced a learning return across age and ability groups, a compensatory formula would weight their allocation to benefit the least favoured. This is more attainable than the broad social change envisaged by current priority schemes and it may speed up the implementation of successful innovations. It would not be too difficult to develop a social priority index that reflected both cost-effectiveness and equity.

3 The next measure is a central one to the redistributive strategy. It involves measuring the costs and benefits of each extra year of education across the spectrum of socio-economic backgrounds. This is one of the most direct ways of achieving equity that compensates not just for the monetary loss but for the different psychological costs associated with social origin, peer group and religion. This is a subjective area, and is not amenable to easy quantification. However, it would be possible to test predictions from diverse models of choice against the actual behaviour of a national sample.

4 While the previous indicators have been concerned with immediate costs and benefits, it is of equal importance to estimate the relative returns on each extra year of education for students of different social origins. As we have seen both the economic and the social rewards of extra education are determined to a large degree by the status of one's parents. 'Objective' sociological indicators of status and economic expectations of educational attainment could, therefore, be formulated and could give some basis to the 'subjective' constraints noted in 3.

5 Finally it would be necessary to monitor the rates at which these indices are changing. In the case of 1, 3 and 4 we would wish to observe an annual decrease in the value of each index. In the case of 2 we might expect to observe the gradual conformity of expenditure in different regions, authorities and districts with the scale of specific priorities.

Conclusions

Education is often considered as a process of achievement and personal growth, and as a means for the enlargement of life chances. Since there are few institutions in urban societies where the individual is so reliant on his own resources, education has been given the job of breaking down the inequalities between ethnic groups, classes and regions. It is supposed to be an agent not only of modernization, but also the legitimator of the inequalities of advanced industrialism. This is far too much to expect of any 'secular religion'. Despite the huge amount of public money that the educational system eats up, the mechanism of selection, allocation and rewards is still not working according to any model of social engineering and probably never will. The logic of this mechanism, as we saw in Chapter 5, is only remotely related to any of the theoretical models of Chapter 1. Any idea then that the sociological dimensions of educational inequality can be greatly reduced, therefore, represents wishful thinking.

It is for this reason that the economic dimensions were proposed as being real and tractable for immediate action. Indirectly, treatment of inequities in this field may rebound on the cultural dimensions of educational inequality and perhaps whittle them away. However, even revolutionary changes in the distribution of wealth and income will not spell the end of the profoundly inegalitarian tendencies of individual learning and attainment. If educational inequality is to be cured we must get beyond both individualism and rhetoric and look at those structures and processes of industrial societies which do not necessarily follow the logic of one's chosen world view. Only when this is done will it be possible to distinguish between those inequalities that are indispensable to productivity and liberty and those historic abuses which could well be swept away.

References and name index

The numbers in italics after each entry refer to page numbers within this book.

Anderson, C. A. (1961) A skeptical note on education and mobility. In A. H. Halsey *et al.* (eds) *Education Economy and Society*. London: Macmillan. *109*

Averch, Harvey (1972) *How Effective is Schooling? A Synthesis of Research Findings*. Santa Monica: Rand Corporation. *61*

Banks, Olive (1976) *The Sociology of Education*. London: Batsford. *76, 99*

Baratz, Stephen S. and Joan C. Baratz (1970) Early childhood intervention: the social science base of institutional racism. *Harvard Educational Review 40:* 29–50. *109*

Bell, Daniel (1972) On meritocracy and equality. *The Public Interest*, Fall 29–68. *117*

Bell, Daniel (1974) *The Coming of Post Industrial Society: A Venture in Social Forecasting*. London: Heinemann. *39, 49*

Berg, Ivar (1970) *Education and Jobs: The Great Training Robbery*. Harmondsworth: Penguin. *50*

Berger, Peter L., Brigitte Berger and Hansfield Kellner (1973)

The Homeless Mind: Modernization and Consciousness. Harmondsworth: Penguin. *122*

Bernstein, Basil (1970) Education cannot compensate for society. *New Society* 26 February. *25, 27, 102–3*

Blaug, Mark (1971) The correlation between education and earnings: what does it signify? *Higher Education* 53–74. *50, 51*

Block, N. J. and Dworkin, Gerald (1974) IQ, heritability and inequality, Parts I and II. *Philosophy and Public Affairs 3*: 331–409; *4:* 40–99. *91*

Boudon, Raymond (1973) *L'Inégalité des chances.* Paris: Libraire Armand, translated (1974) *Education, Opportunity and Social Inequality.* London: John Wiley. *106, 110, 124*

Boudon, Raymond (1975) For a better understanding of the relationship between education and equality in France. Discussion paper given at the OECD Seminar on *Education, Inequality and Life Chances.* Paris. 2 Vols. *1*: 293–307. *124*

Bourdieu, Pierre and Jean-Claude Passeron (1970) *La Reproduction: éléments pour une théorie du système d'enseignement.* Paris: Editions de Minuit. *112*

Bourdieu, Pierre and Jean-Claude Passeron (1973) Cultural reproduction and social reproduction. In Richard Brown (ed.) *Knowledge, Education and Cultural Change.* London. Tavistock. *102*

Bourdieu, Pierre and Monique Saint-Martin (1974) Scholastic excellence and the values of the educational system. In John Eggleston (ed.) *Contemporary Research in the Sociology of Education.* London: Methuen. *45*

Bowles, Samuel (1972) *The Genetic Inheritance of IQ and the Intergenerational Reproduction of Economic Inequality.* Harvard: Institute of Economic Research Discussion Paper No. 253. Mimeo. *97*

Bowles, Samuel and Herbert Gintis (1972–3) IQ in the U.S. class structure.*Social Policy* Nov/Dec 1972 and Jan/Feb 1973: 65–96. *94*

Bowles, Samuel (1973) Understanding unequal economic opportunity. *American Economic Review* (Proceedings) *63*: 346–56. *94*

Bowles, Samuel and Herbert Gintis (1976) *Schooling in Capitalist America.* London: Routledge and Kegan Paul. *57, 94*

Bowman, Mary Jean (1966) The human investment revolution in economic thought. *Sociology of Education 39:* 111–37. *24*

Bowman, Mary Jean (1975) Education and opportunity: some economic perspectives. *Oxford Review of Education 1*: 73–89. *119*

Boyd, David (1973) *Elites and their Education.* Slough: National Foundation for Educational Research. *45*

Burt, Cyril (1959) Class differences in general intelligence: III. *The British Journal of Statistical Psychology 12*: 15–33. *22*

Burt, Cyril (1961) Intelligence and social mobility. *British Journal of Statistical Psychology 14*: 3–24. *86, 92*

Byrne, David, Bill Williamson and Barbara Fletcher (1975) *The Poverty of Education: A Study in the Politics of Opportunity*. London: Martin Robertson. *64*

Coleman, James S. *et al.* (1966) *Report on Equality of Educational Opportunity (EEOS)*. U.S. Government Printing Office for Department of Health, Education and Welfare. *26*

Collins, Randall (1971) Functional and conflict theories of educational stratification. *American Sociological Review 36*: 1002–19. *45*

Cronbach, Lee J. (1973) Five decades of controversy over mental testing. In Charles Frankel (ed.) *Social Science Controversies and Public Policy Decisions*. Paper presented at a Conference sponsored by the American Academy of Arts and Sciences. *79*

Crowder, N. David (1974) A critique of Duncan's stratification research. *Sociology 8*: 19–45. *41, 42*

Crowther Commission (1959–60) *15 to 18: Report of the Central Advisory Council for Education – England*. 2 vols. (Surveys). London: HMSO. *22–3, 83, 97, 103*

Cox, C. B. and A. E. Dyson (eds) (1969–70) *Black Papers One, Two and Three*. London: Critical Quarterly Society. *14, 15*

Cox, C. B. and Rhodes Boyson (eds) (1975) *Black Paper: The Fight for Education*. London: Dent. *14, 15*

Davies, Brian and B. Bernstein (1969) Some sociological comments on Plowden. In R. Peters (ed.) *Perspectives on Plowden*, London: Routledge and Kegan Paul. *57*

Davies, Brian (1976) *Social Control and Education*. London: Methuen. *103*

Davis, Kingsley and W. E. Moore (1945) Some principles of stratification. *American Sociological Review 10*: 242–9. *127*

Diamond, Lord (1975) *Royal Commission on the Distribution of Income and Wealth*. Report No. 1. London: HMSO. *47*

Douglas, J. W. B. (1964) The Home and the School. London: MacGibbon and Kee. *22, 61*

Douglas, J. W. B. (1973) A blunt instrument. *New Society 25*: 572.

Douglas, J. W. B., J. M. Ross and H. R. Simpson (1968) *All Our Future: A Longitudinal Study of Secondary Education*. London: Davies.

Duncan, Beverley (1968) Trends in output and distribution in

schooling. In E. B. Sheldon and W. E. Moore, *Indicators of Social Change*. New York: Russell Sage Foundation. *37*
Duncan, O. D., David L. Featherman and Beverly Duncan (1972) *Socio-economic Background and Achievement*. London: Seminar Press. *31, 42, 56, 97*
Early Leaving (1954) Report of the Minister of Education's Central Advisory Council. London: HMSO.

Eckland, Bruce K. (1972) Comments on school effects, gene-environment covariance and the heritability of intelligence. In L. Ehrmann, G. Omenn and E. Caspari, *Genetics, Environment and Behaviour: Implications for Educational Policy*. New York: Academic Press.
Engels, Frederick (1913–14) On authority. In *Die Neue Zeit*. Vol. 23, Band 1. *52*
Eggleston, John (ed.) (1974) *Contemporary Research in the Sociology of Education*. London: Methuen. *64*
Eggleston, John (1975) Resarch and the comprehensives. *Times Educational Supplement* 28 February. *69*
Eicher, Jean-Claude and Alain Mingat (1975) Education and equality in France. Paper given at the OECD Seminar on *Education, Inequality and Life Chances*. 2 Vols. Paris. *1*: 202–92. *125*
Eliot, T. S. (1948) *Notes towards the Definition of Culture*. London: Faber. *77*
Eltis, Walter (1975) How public sector growth causes balance of payments deficits. *International Currency Review* Jan/Feb. 27–30. *40*
Eysenck, H. J. (1971) *Race, Intelligence and Education*. London: Temple Smith.
Eysenck, H. J. (1973) The triumph of the average. *New Society* 25 October. 201–3. *93*
Eysenck, H. J. (1973) *The Inequality of Man*. London: Temple Smith. *86, 93*
Eysenck, H. J. (1975) Equality and education: fact and fiction. *Oxford Review of Education 1*: 51–8.

Field, Frank (1974) *Unequal Britain: A Report on the Cycle of Inequality*. London: Arrow Books. *47*
Fisher, J. (1959) The twisted pear and the prediction of behaviour. *Journal of Consulting Psychology 23*: 400–5. *83*
Floud, J., A. H. Halsey and F. M. Martin (1956) *Social Class and Educational Opportunity*. London: Heinemann. *22*
Floud, Jean (1961) Reserves of ability. *Forum 3*(2): 66–8. *23, 83*

Folger, John K. and Charles B. Nam. (1964) Trends in education in relation to occupational structure. *Sociology of Education 38*: 19–33. *37*

Ford, Julienne (1969) *Social Class and the Comprehensive School*. London: Routledge and Kegan Paul. *23, 29, 68*

General Household Survey (1973) *Introductory Report: An Interdepartmental Survey Sponsored by the Central Statistical Office*. Office of Population Censuses and Surveys. London: HMSO. *37, 40–1, 48*

Giddens, A. (1973) *The Class Structure of the Advanced Societies*. London: Hutchinson. *38*

Glass, D. V. (ed.) (1954) *Social Mobility in Britain*. London: Routledge and Kegan Paul.

Glennerster, H. (1972) Education and inequality. In P. Townsend and N. Bosanquet (eds) *Labour and Inequality*. London: Fabian Society. *118*

Halsey, A. H. (1958) Genetics, social structure, and intelligence. *British Journal of Sociology 9*: 15–28. *22*

Halsey, A. H. and Ivor Crewe (1967) *Social Survey of the Civil Service*. Evidence submitted to the Committee under the Chairmanship of Lord Fulton, Vol. III (1). London: HMSO. *45*

Halsey, A. H. (1972) *Educational Priority*. London: HMSO. *62, 67*

Halsey, A. H. (1974) Students' comings and goings. *Times Higher Education Supplement* 13 September. 2. *38*

Halsey, A. H. (1975a) Sociology and the equality debate. *Oxford Review of Education 1*: 9–23. *21, 39, 117*

Halsey, A. H. (1975b) Education and social mobility in Britain since World War II. Paper given at the OECD Seminar on *Education, Inequality and Life Chances*. *97*. 2 Vols. Paris. *1*: 501–9. *38, 42, 57, 68, 119*

Herrnstein, Richard J. (1971) IQ – *Atlantic Monthly 228*:43–64. *13, 15, 93*

Herrnstein, Richard J. (1973) *IQ in the Meritocracy*. Boston: Atlantic Press. *13, 18, 30*

Hyman, Herbert (1953) The values systems of different classes: a social psychological contribution to the analysis of stratification. In Bendix and Lipsett (1966) (eds) *Class Status and Power*. Glencoe, Ill.: Free Press. *105*

Illich, Ivan (1970) *Deschooling Society*. Harmondsworth: Penguin. *25*

Jackson, Robert and A. H. Halsey (1972–3) Debate on equality and community. *Times Educational Supplement* 20 October, 3 November, 1 December, 22 December and 4 January. *123*
Jencks, Christopher *et al.* (1972) *Inequality: A Re-assessment of the Effect of Family and Schooling in America.* New York: Basic Books. *18, 28, 30, 42, 48, 59, 61, 63, 64, 66, 70, 73, 82, 83, 87, 89, 93*
Jensen, Arthur R. (1967) Estimation of the limits of heritability of traits by comparison of monozygotic and dyzygotic twins. *Proceedings of the National Academy of Science 58*: 149–56. *85*
Jensen, Arthur R. (1969) How much can we boost IQ and scholastic achievement? *Harvard Educational Review 39*: 1–123. *28, 80*
Jensen, Arthur R. (1975) The price of inequality. *Oxford Review of Education 1*: 59–71. *89*
Jensen, Arthur R. (1976) *Educability and Group Differences.* London: Methuen. *90*

Karier, Clarence (1972) Testing for order and control in the corporate liberal state. *Educational Theory 22*: 154–80. *79*
Keddie, Nell (ed.) (1973) *Tinker Tailor . . .: The Myth of Cultural Deprivation.* Harmondsworth: Penguin Education. *73*
Keller, Suzanne and Marisa Zavalloni (1964) Ambition and social class: a respecification. *Social Forces 43*: 58–70. *105, 106*
Kelsall, R. K. (1957) *Application for Admission to Universities.* A Report to the Association of the Universities of the British Commonwealth. London. *45*
Kennett, John (1973) The sociology of Pierre Bourdieu. *Educational Review 25*: 237–49. *112*
Kerckhoff, Alan C. (1974) Stratification processes and outcomes in England and the U.S. *American Sociological Review 39*: 789–801. *58, 66, 69, 97*
King, Ronald (1974) Social class, educational attainment and provision: an L.E.A. case study. *Policy and Politics 3*: 17–35. *56*

Labov, William (1969) The logic of non-standard English. In Nell Keddie (ed.) *Tinker Tailor . . .: The Myth of Cultural Deprivation.* Harmondsworth: Penguin Education. *27, 102*
Lane, Michael (1972) Explaining educational choice. *Sociology 6*: 255–66. *107*
Layard, P. R. *et al.* (1971) *Qualified Manpower and Economic Performance.* London: Allen Lane. *50*
Layard, Richard (1974) *On Measuring the Redistribution of Lifetime Income.* In M. F. Feldstein and R. P. Inman (eds) (1976) *Economics of Public Services.* London: Macmillan.

Little, A. and J. Westergaard (1964) The trend of class differentials in educational opportunity in England and Wales. *British Journal of Sociology 15*: 301–16. *22, 66*
Little, A. (1971) A sociological portrait: education. *New Society*. 1245–8. *54*
Lynn, Richard (1969) Comprehensives and equality: the quest for the unattainable. In C. B. Cox and A. F. Dyson (eds), *Black Paper Two*. Critical Quarterly Society. *85–6*

Maynard, Alan (1975) *An Experiment with Choice in Education*. London: Institute of Economic Affairs. Hobart Paper 64. *125*
Merrett, A. J. (1975) Money down the drain. *Times Educational Supplement*. 25 July. 2. *127*
Montagu, Ashley (ed.) (1975) *Race and IQ*. London: Oxford University Press.
Moynihan, Daniel P. (1972) Equalizing education – in whose benefit. *The Public Interest* Fall, 69–89. *55*

Newsom Report (1963) *Half our Future*. London: HMSO. *13, 56*

OECD (1969a) *Statistics on the Occupational Structure of the Labour Force in 53 Countries*. Paris. *40*
OECD (1969b) *Development in Secondary Education: Trends and Implications*. Paris. *37*

Peaker, Gilbert F. (1967) The regression analysis of the national survey. *Plowden Report*, Vol. 2, Appendix 4. London: HMSO. *59*
Peaker, Gilbert F. (1971) *The Plowden Children Four Years Later*. Slough: National Foundation for Educational Research.
Plowden Report (1967) *Children and their Primary Schools*. Central Advisory Council for Education. London: HMSO. *26, 59*
Psacharapoulos, G. (1971) Rates of return to investment in education around the world. *Comparative Education Review 16*: 54–67. *40*
Public Schools Commission (1968) *Report*. London: HMSO. *56*

Rawls, John (1971) *A Theory of Justice*. Oxford: Clarendon Press. *116–17*
Ridge, John (ed.) (1974) *Mobility in Britain Reconsidered*. Oxford Studies in Social Mobility Working Paper 2. Oxford: Clarendon. *46, 66, 74, 97, 111*
Runciman, W. G. (1967) 'Social' equality. *Philsophical Quarterly* 17. *122*

Robbins Report (1963) Committee on Higher Education. London: HMSO. *22–24, 61*

Rosen, Harold (1973) *Language and Class*. Bristol: Falling Wall Press. *25, 102*

Rosenthal, R. and L. Jacobson (1968) *Pygmalion in the Classroom*. New York: Holt, Rinehart and Winston. *26*

Ross, J. *et al*. (1972) *A Critical Appraisal of Comprehensive Education*. Slough: National Foundation of Educational Research. *56*

Simon, Brian (1960) *Studies in the History of Education 1780–1870*. London: Laurence and Wishart. *21*

Social Policy (1972–3) Editorial. The lingering infatuation with IQ. Nov/Dec., Jan/Feb. *94*

Svalastoga, Kaare (1964) Social differentiation. In R. E. Faris (ed.), *Handbook of Modern Sociology*, New York: Rand McNally. *103*

Svalastoga, Kaare (1965) Social mobility: the Western European model. *Acta Sociologica 9*: 175–82. *46*

Tawney, R. H. (1931) *Equality*. London: Allen and Unwin. *13*

Thurow, Lester (1972) Education and economic equality. *The Public Interest*. Summer. 66–81. *47–48*

Tizard, Jack (1975) Race and IQ: the limits of probability. *New Behaviour 1:* 6–9. *89*

Treiman, Donald J. and Kermit Terrell (1975) The process of status attainment in the U.S. and Great Britain. *American Journal of Sociology 81*: 563–83. *71, 73, 96, 111*

Tuck, Mary G. (1974) The effect of different factors on the level of academic achievement in England and Wales. *Social Science Research 3:* 141–50. *63*

Turner, Ralph H. (1960) Sponsored and contest mobility and the school system. *American Sociological Review 25:* 855–67. *58*

Westoby, Adam, David Webster and Gareth Williams (1976) *Social Scientists at Work*. Guildford: Society for Research in Higher Education. *110*

White Paper on Educational Reconstruction (1943). In J. Stuart Maclure (ed.), (1973) *Educational Documents: England and Wales*. London: Chapman and Hall. *20*

Willmott, P. (ed.) (1976) *Sharing Inflation? Poverty Report*. London: Temple Smith. *47*

Wilson, Bryan (ed.) (1975) *Education, Equality and Society*. London: Allen and Unwin. *77*

Young, Michael (1958) *The Rise of the Meritocracy 1870–2033*. London: Penguin. *84*

Subject index